CONDUCTING EFFECTIVE NEGOTIATIONS

How To Books on business and management

Arranging Insurance	Managing Credit
Be a Freelance Sales Agent	Managing Meetings
Buy & Run a Shop	Managing Projects
Buy & Run a Small Hotel	Managing Yourself
Cash from Your Computer	Market Yourself
Collecting a Debt	Master Public Speaking
Communicate at Work	Mastering Book-Keeping
Conducting Effective Interviews	Mastering Business English
Conducting Effective Negotiations	Organising Effective Training
Conducting Staff Appraisals	Preparing a Business Plan
Coping with Self Assessment	Publish a Book
Counsel People at work	Publish a Newsletter
Dealing with Your Bank	Raise Business Finance
Delivering Customer Service	Sell Your Business
Do Your Own Advertising	Setting up Your Own Limited Company
Do Your Own PR	Start a Business from Home
Doing Business Abroad	Start Your Own Business
Doing Business on the Internet	Starting to Manage
Employ & Manage Staff	Successful Mail Order Marketing
Investing in People	Taking on Staff
Investing in Stocks & Shares	Understand Finance at Work
Keep Business Accounts	Using the Internet
Manage a Sales Team	Winning Presentations
Manage an Office	Write a Press Release
Manage Computers at Work	Write & Sell Computer Software
Manage People at Work	Writing a Report
Managing Budgets & Cash Flows	Writing Business Letters

Further titles in preparation

The How To Series now contains more than 200 titles in the following categories:

Business Basics	Mind & Body
Family Reference	Student Handbooks
Jobs & Careers	Successful Writing
Living & Working Abroad	

Please send for a free copy of the latest catalogue for full details (see back cover for address).

BUSINESS BASICS

CONDUCTING EFFECTIVE NEGOTIATIONS

How to get the deal you want

Patrick Forsyth

WITHDRAWN FROM STOCK

How To Books

Acknowledgements

No one writes a book of this sort without drawing on many influences and experiences. In describing negotiation I am particularly grateful to those with whom I have been involved in a training context over the years – both clients and their course participants. I would also like to acknowledge my time with the Marketing Improvements Group which introduced me to the world of consultancy and training and gave me so much valuable experience. My first work involving negotiation was done whilst there, and my style of explaining it no doubt still draws on material originally drawn together while working with them, and reflects the contributions of many people. I am grateful for their assistance.

P.F.

Cartoons by Mike Flanagan

British Library Cataloguing in Publication Data
A catalogue record for this book is available from the British Library.

© Copyright 1997 by Patrick Forsyth

First published in 1997 by How To Books Ltd, 3 Newtec Place,
Magdalen Road, Oxford OX4 1RE, United Kingdom.
Tel: (01865) 793806. Fax: (01865) 248780.

Produced for How To Books by Deer Park Productions.

Typeset by Anneset, Weston-super-Mare, Somerset.
Printed and bound by Cromwell Press, Broughton Gifford, Melksham, Wiltshire.

Contents

Contents

List of Illustrations

Preface

Everyone negotiates: in the office or work situation, or over the garden fence. It is not something only other people do, it is a core skill valuable to all of us and vital to many.

This book is about negotiating – bargaining – and doing so successfully. Negotiation is a **communications skill**, one that overlaps, indeed leads on from, **persuasive communication.** Negotiation is concerned with the relationship between two parties where the needs of both are largely in balance. For instance, in the classic case of wage bargaining, the employer wants to reach an agreement, to secure his workforce and keep his business running, and the employees want an agreement, so that once the process of negotiation is over they can get on with earning at the new rate. This principle of balance of need effectively defines the process.

Imagine you want a new car. You visit a car showroom. To begin with you are undecided about which model to buy. The salesman is, therefore, at this stage **selling** to you: a process of persuasive communication. Once you have made up your mind – though you may not tell the salesman that you have – you are concerned with arranging the best deal – the finance, extras, discounts and so on – and the process of bargaining begins.

Persuasive communication is simply about *getting what you want.* Negotiation is about making the best possible deal: getting what you want in the best possible way. It is a technique which can help you make better deals.

Have you noticed that the way people go about the process of negotiation affects the outcome? The expression of someone 'running rings' around someone is truly descriptive. Some people always seem to manage this, others do it less effectively. This is because negotiation is a skill. It can be learnt, and with practice, you can be the one running the rings around others. It is a skill which can smooth relations, and save you time, money, aggravation and face. It is of use in many business situations, and in your social life.

The types of circumstances calling for negotiation are vast. They include:

- Negotiating as you sell. You do not need to be in a commercial organisation to have to sell, still less just to be persuasive.

- Negotiating as a buyer or purchaser.

- Negotiating the terms and conditions of employment, or organisational matters.

- Negotiating any matter where the details of arrangements between two or more parties may have to be thrashed out and agreed.

Negotiating includes discussions between colleagues, or people you do not know, between people in the same organisation or different ones, between people of different backgrounds, nationalities and outlooks. It may be lengthy and formal, or short and transient. Whatever the circumstances, being able to negotiate effectively can make an important difference to the outcome of the discussions.

There is a catch, but it is not a prohibitive one. It is simply that to be an effective negotiator you need to learn something about the **process** and the **skills** involved, then practise them. This book is designed to help you make a start. By thinking about, and practising the principles and techniques that the book reviews, you can begin to put yourself in a position to do better in many bargaining situations.

I want you to buy this book. You want to be a more effective negotiator. This book will help you do just that. Buy it and we both get what we want. Is it a deal?

Patrick Forsyth
Touchstone Training & Consultancy
17 Clocktower Mews
London N1 7BB

1
Understanding Negotiation

'When a man tells me he is going to put all his cards on the table, I always look up his sleeve.'

Lord Hore-Belisha

NEGOTIATING IN CONTEXT

Why would we want to learn how to negotiate effectively? And what makes it such a complex skill? To answer these questions we need to understand exactly what negotiation is and how it works.

In so many discussions the conclusions cannot be a simple 'yes' or 'no'. There will always be many permutations and aspects to be discussed, which have to add up to an 'outcome' acceptable to both, or all, parties. The process of achieving this may well take some time. Each aspect has to be considered in turn; and, of course, different people have different ideas about what they want, what is reasonable and how to go about achieving agreement.

RECOGNISING THE ADVERSARIAL ASPECT

There is certainly an adversarial aspect to negotiation. Both parties want to win. One of the tricks of successful negotiation, therefore, is for it to end with both sides feeling they have done well – so called 'win–win' negotiation. The adversarial element must be kept in check so that negotiation doesn't deteriorate into a slanging match, with both sides setting impossible conditions and no agreement likely.

Achieving give and take

Negotiating involves a fair bit of give and take. You cannot proceed without having an understanding of the other party and their objectives. Ultimately we are after the best deal which is possible, rather than chasing an unrealistic ideal. None of this happens without the process of to and fro discussion taking on something of a ritualistic element. There are conventions, ways of doing things and unless we keep reasonably close to the fabric of the process, real progress might be jeopardised.

LEARNING THE TECHNIQUES

By learning and deploying the techniques of negotiation you will save yourself or your organisation time and money. Or you may simply put yourself in a stonger position to achieve what you want in discussion.

Several factors make for success; we will review them in turn. The first, basic yet most vital factor is that negotiation is a form of communication. Make no mistake: if you do not communicate clearly you will never be a successful negotiator

Linking persuasive communication and negotiation

Making things clear
Communication – making something clear – is never easy. Persuasive communication – getting someone to do what we want – can be downright difficult. Negotiation – agreeing the 'deal' – is something else. The processes overlap, as shown in Figure 1. Before we get into the details about negotiation we must set the scene and deal with the basic skills from which it springs.

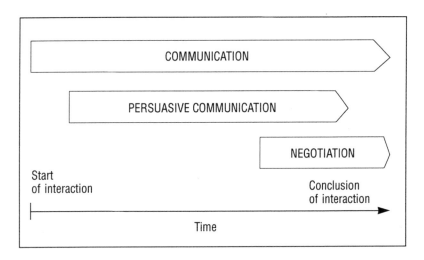

Fig. 1. Negotiation in context.

Day-to-day communication

Communication may *seem* easy. We do it all the time, with family, friends and day-to-day contacts of all sorts as well as in a business context. Communication may be verbal or in writing. But communication may have inherent complications, such as the telephone; this poses problems because you cannot see people and judge their intentions or reactions from facial expressions. Such communication may be emotional, complex or hasty.

Avoiding communications breakdown

Whatever form it takes communication may run into problems because it is:

- unclear
- imprecise
- or full of jargon.

There are dozens of potential hazards; you may lose the thread of your argument, or the other person may not be listening

Classic examples of communication breakdown abound. A nice example of simple confusion is the sign in a shop that says 'Ears Pierced While You Wait'. The late American President, Richard Nixon, is credited with the following convoluted statement: 'I know that you think you understand what you think I said, but I am not sure you realise that what you heard is not what I meant'. You are certainly going to need to be clearer than that!

If people are not clear about what you mean, you cannot hope to move on to the next stage: of *persuading* them.

Clear communication is the first foundation for successful negotiation.

Being persuasive

If communication is *clear*, it can then be made *persuasive*. Being persuasive, in turn, depends on the right approach. And this must be based on the point of view, and thinking, of the *other* person. It is very easy for communication to end up unpersuasive because it is no more than our saying 'do this', with no consideration of the other person or their point of view. We want action but only because the other person understands, appreciates and sees the need for it.

Understanding other people
While we need to state *our* case and regard it as *our* communication, we will only get our way if people on the receiving end find it acceptable. If they believe we are trying to do something *to* them, to persuade them against their will, agreement will be difficult. On the other hand, if they feel we have their interests in mind it will be easier.

Start by considering the thinking process involved when considering another's request for action. Based on psychological studies in America, this process is often described as one that moves through seven stages:

1. I am important and I want to be respected.
2. Consider my needs.
3. How will your ideas/proposition help me?
4. What are the facts?
5. What are the snags?
6. What shall I do?
7. I approve (or not).

Weighing up the case
This seems like common sense. Indeed, it is what you do in all manner of situations in which a decision needs to be made. You 'weigh up' the case or argument, put all the good points on one side, all the less good on the other and assess the net effect (see Figure 2).

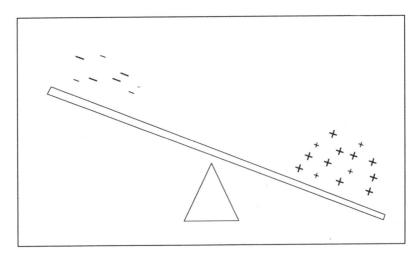

Fig. 2. Weighing up the case.

Examining the decision-making process

Any attempt at communication that results in an unsatisfactory response to any of the seven stages outlined above is unlikely to end in agreement. The mind must be satisfied on each point before considering the next. To be successful the persuasive process must match, and run parallel with, the decision-making sequence. Figure 3 shows how both sides relate and what their objectives are at each stage.

Decision Sequence	Persuasion Objectives	Persuasion Stages
I am important Consider my needs	To create rapport, generate interest or acceptance. To find out about them	1. Opening
What are the facts?	To state a case that will be seen as balanced in favour of action	2. Stating the case
What are the snags?	Preventing or handling negative reactions that may unbalance the argument	3. Handling objections
What shall I do? I approve	Obtaining a commitment to action, or to a step in the right direction	4. Injunction to act

Fig. 3. The decision-making process.

Among the many techniques of persuasion, matching the other person's decision-making thoughts, and describing your own case in a way that reflects that, are key.

Persuasion may fail if the detail here is not respected. The sequence and the totality of the process must be accommodated, and the pace at which the decider is going broadly matched. Going too fast can be self-defeating and result in a 'don't push me' response. The aim is always a *commitment to act*, or to achieve a firm step on the way to the ultimate goal.

Example

A secretary wants her boss to buy her a new and better word processor. Her ultimate objective is for him to say 'yes, buy it' about a particular machine. A useful step may be to persuade him to review some brochures, arrange and attend a demonstration or obtain a firm quotation. All such steps can be the basis of specific objectives: she may decide that the first thing to do is to get him to agree to a demonstration.

Sometimes there are many such steps to be gone through before the ultimate objective is reached. Getting agreement to each of these becomes a worthwhile goal in itself.

Thinking ahead

Whatever the ultimate objective, part of what ensures persuasion works is thinking ahead. Anticipate how the decision will be made, what factors are most important. Questioning techniques will be important to this process.

A chain of events

A successful outcome does not always emerge from one contact between everyone involved. Several meetings or exchanges may be necessary. When there is a multiplicity of contacts, each stage has its own sequence to be followed, as does the whole process.

Anticipating responses

There is always a need to plan ahead if communication is to run smoothly and objectives are to be achieved. Although you cannot predict exactly what responses will be, anticipating as accurately as possible will always help. This does not imply adopting a 'scripted' or parrot-like approach. Rather it means that you intend to direct the conversation towards a specific conclusion.

Keeping on course

It may help to think of this graphically. Imagine the helmsman of a yacht, sailing across an open sea and subject to the impact of wind and tide. He might take a number of courses, though imagining a straight line to the chosen destination will allow him to correct course and keep on track.

Another issue must be touched on. It should already be clear that, if persuasion is to succeed, it is necessary to tackle the communication with a clear eye on the listener and their point of view. The whole approach must come over as *acceptable* and not – by seeming overassertive or even aggressive – switch people off. So, the next issue is making things acceptable.

Projecting an acceptable manner

Two factors combine to make your manner acceptable:

- **projection**
- **empathy**.

Projection means the way we come over to others, particularly the confidence, credibility and 'clout' we convey. Empathy simply means the ability to put yourself in the other person's shoes and see things from their point of view: not only to see them, but to *be seen* to do so.

Recognising different types of communicator

We can consider four distinct types of communicator on an axis of high and low projection, and high and low empathy. This is illustrated in Figure 4.

Type 1
The **high pressure** communicator is over-aggressive and insensitive. *They* may feel they win the argument, but their projection without empathy becomes self-defeating and swtiches people off. The archetypal high-pressure communicator is the popular image of, say, the double-glazing salesman.

Type 2
The **take it or leave it communicator** has little interest in either the other person or even his own ideas. A lack of commitment to the whole process tends to let it run into the sand. The archetypal take it or leave it communicator is the unhelpful shop assistant.

Type 3
The **weak communicator** is the sort of which it is said disparagingly, 'they mean well'. And so they do. They have good sensitivity to the other people; they come over as essentially nice. However, they tend to take the side of the listener so much that persuasion vanishes and they achieve no commitment.

Type 4
The **ideal communicator** has a creative understanding of the listener. He is well informed and produces both agreement and commitment to the satisfaction of both sides. Being seen to see the other person's point of view is itself crucial.

Fig. 4. Types of communicator.

Achieving the correct blend of empathy and projection is important. Both elements are necessary, but either can be under- or overdone. If the combination is right the other person will find it reasonable and acceptable. It is not only important to communication and persuasiveness, but is also the approach that you will need if you are to negotiate successfully.

Clearly there is more to being persuasive than this. Exactly *how* one goes through the seven stages of consideration, and the techniques involved, are also important.

Persuasive communication is the second foundation for successful negotiation.

MOVING ON TOWARDS NEGOTIATION

Only when someone is persuaded in principle towards a particular course of action will they be interested in moving on to make any sort of deal. If you have communicated clearly and achieved understanding, if you have succeeded in being truly persuasive and there is essentially agreement to proceed, then you can move on to the process of negotiation.

In real life the processes of persuasion and negotiation overlap. There is no sharp division. Often a complete cycle of interaction takes place, as was shown in Figure 1, with communication going on throughout. Whilst the approach described, operating from the basis of a sound appreciation of the other person's point of view, is the beginning of effectiveness in this area, there is clearly more to it than that.

The process of communication needs working at; that of persuasive communication even more so. It must be made manageable. It needs planning and structuring. It must be deployed with an acute consciousness of what is going on, because we never know how people will react.

CHECKLIST

1. Negotiation is itself a form of communication, and one that depends on clear and often persuasive communication. Securing such a foundation is the first step to being successful.

2. Making negotiation a give-and-take process is most likely to secure the best deal.

3. While negotiation is essentially adversarial, adopting a 'win-win' approach will help bring it to a satisfactory conclusion.

4. Negotiation is an interactive skill. You must be as concerned with what others are doing as you are about yourself to be a successful negotiator.

5. Negotiation is complex, but the techniques that make it work can be learned. Anyone prepared to approach it in a considered manner can give themselves an edge in bargaining.

CASE STUDY

The situation below relates to a charity organisation. Its focus is on raising money for its cause and internal costs must be kept down. Staffing is therefore tight. Recent changes have included moving the catalogue operation, selling everything from Christmas cards to gifts, from a second site into the main building.

Paul makes a complaint

Paul runs the catalogue order office. One of his main preoccupations is customer service, and he finds that the switchboard is not servicing his department efficiently. Despite having a note explaining who handles what, the switchboard is misrouting many calls, constant transfer is then necessary and customers are upset. This is especially important in a charity as any inefficiency is quickly associated with waste of money.

Paul writes a memo to the Administration Manager complaining that the lack of efficiency is upsetting customers, risking losing orders and revenue, and diluting the organisation's good image.

Rita is defensive

Rita is the Administration Manager. She is busy, especially so with the changes and the seemingly endless need to keep staffing tight. She has only met Paul once, when his department moved in, and has little knowledge of his part of the overall operation.

Rita knows the switchboard operators are hard pressed. She defends them strongly, suggesting Paul takes steps to better inform customers about who they should ask for. She returns to what she sees as more pressing matters, hoping no more action will be necessary.

The situation and problem remain and Paul decides a meeting is needed to sort the matter out.

Achieving a resolution

As Paul thinks about the meeting his objective is clear: service must be improved. He quickly realises, however, that it is not a matter of instructions, or even of persuasion. He has to work with Rita and accepts that establishing smooth relations between them is also an objective. He realises that attitudes have caused the problem to escalate because:

1. He saw the situation as a simple instruction: make the change.

2. She saw only the criticism and became defensive, leaving the ball in Paul's court.

Paul realises he must negotiate. First class standards of service are vital. But the switchboard operators probably do have a problem. After all, coping additionally with the catalogue department has perhaps doubled the number of calls they take.

There needs to be some give and take. It is an 'if ... then ...' situation. Paul begins to list what he could do:

(a) Prepare an easy check reference to go in front of each operator, showing who does what.

(b) Brief the switchboard operators personally on the action necessary.

(c) Explain the importance of these new calls. After all, they give the operators a chance to influence fund raising very directly: good service meaning more orders.

(d) Check the order forms to see whether amendments could make things clearer in future.

(e) Offer to keep the two groups of staff in touch. Perhaps the switchboard operators could each have a tour of the order office to show them what goes on there, and how they are really part of the same team.

In return Paul needs to ask for some priority for customer calls, at the expense of certain other tasks. It is not yet clear what this might involve but it might even call for some reorganisation. There is a balance to be struck, which is why Paul needs to think about what concessions he may offer. Perhaps the first job is to persuade Rita that it is potentially a 'win-win' situation. Despite the immediate aggravations the situation poses for her, in the long term more job interest and motivation could be created.

Both parties will come out of the ensuring exchange better if they avoid reacting precipitately or emotionally and see the situation for what it is: negotiation. If their discussions take this approach then a solution is likely to be satisfactory to everyone.

DISCUSSION POINTS

1. Why is understanding how negotiation relates to communication generally, and persuasive communication in particular, so important?

2. Why is communicating clearly such an important component of negotiation?

3. What are the situations in which you might have to negotiate in future? These are worth listing to have in mind as we continue.

2
Deploying the Fundamental Techniques

'Poker playing is not to be learnt in one evening.'

Anon

DEFINING THE PROCESS

There is more to negotiating than may at first meet the eye. Consider what negotiation is *not*. It is not simply stating a grievance. Imagine the toaster has come back from the mender's and is still doing a good impression of a crematorium. It would be most people's instinct to complain, but often without proposing a remedy. At best, complaints produce apologies. At worst, they produce arguments in which threats produce counter-threats, and even an impasse.

All too often communication can end up this way. It starts with a complaint: 'Productivity in your department is dropping', 'Sales results are below target,' and deteriorates into an argument: 'No, it's not', 'There are good reasons for that' and so on.

What you really want in such circumstances is action. You have to suggest, or prompt, a **proposal**: something that will put things right. Arguments cannot be negotiated, only proposals can. This, in turn, demands that emotions are kept under control. Negotiation is a delicate process which needs thinking about carefully – both before and during it.

Win-win dealing

It is inherent to the process of negotiation that *both* the parties involved end up feeling satisfied that an appropriate deal has been struck. It may not be exactly the result they hoped for, but it is one they can realistically agree to. It is this outcome that gives rise to the description of a win-win negotiating situation. Some individuals feel they must win every point, deliberately creating a win-lose approach. Negotiation is, however, a process of some give and take, and if both parties accept this a win-win approach is more likely to achieve a productive conclusion.

Looking at the implications
Some of the implications of win-win negotiation are shown below.

1. The emphasis should be on seeking common ground, rather than fighting for your way on everything.

2. Relating to the other party and their concerns, rather than just objecting to them.

3. Readiness to compromise, at least to some degree, rather than remaining inflexible.

4. Discussion must accommodate to and fro debate, rather than insist on a rigid agenda.

5. Discussion should include questioning – and thus *listening* – rather than just giving statements of your case.

6. Appropriate information should be disclosed, rather than maintaining total secretiveness.

7. Building relationships, rather than bad feelings with parties is important.

8. The aim is agreement not stalemate.

A win-win conclusion should normally be your aim.

Complexities demand care
Negotiation is a complex process. Several elements need to be borne in mind if the process is to move along satisfactorily.

Negotiation is the process of identifying, arranging and agreeing the terms and conditions, whatever they may be, of a deal.

Remember that persuasive communication starts the process. This is where one party puts across their case and the other begins, in their own mind, to accept it.

As agreement in principle begins to emerge the question switches from 'Will this person agree?', to 'On what *basis* will they agree?'. Each party is then concerned that every detail making up the deal will suit them as much as possible. It may be impossible for both to be satisfied one hundred per cent on every factor – indeed this probably will be so – but the balance must be right.

TRADING AND USING VARIABLES

The different factors that are the raw material of negotiation are called **variables**. They may indeed be many and various, and this fact contributes to the overall complexity of the negotiation process. An everyday example will illustrate the point.

Trading variables in everyday life

Imagine you are going to make some major household purchase: a refrigerator, perhaps. Which model you buy, and from where, will depend on a number of factors – perhaps a surprisingly large number. There is price, of course. But there are also factors about the fridge itself: the star rating of its freezer unit, the size, number and arrangements of shelves, bottle-holding capacity, the colour, which way the door opens, and so on. There may be other, less obvious factors. How much does it cost to run? Will they deliver it, by when and with what certainty? Will they carry it up to a third floor apartment? What payment terms are available? What guarantee and service arrangements apply? You can no doubt think of more.

This kind of purchase may consist only of checking and considering such factors and then making a decision, but some of the factors may not be fixed. Some will be offered – or not – by the shop, others have to be suggested and negotiated. You only get certain things included in the deal when they have been raised, discussed and agreed. Once this process is involved then balance is necessary. Both parties may need to give as well as take.

- You agree to delay delivery by two weeks, and they will deliver free of charge, when they have a van coming your way.

- They agree to knock, say, ten per cent off the price if you agree to pay cash. And so on.

In other words you 'trade' variables. You swop aspects of them to balance and re-balance the deal. Such trading may use all or part of a variable: for instance, you might agree to collect the fridge above, foregoing any kind of delivery, but in return for more discount. The techniques of trading variables will be investigated further as we progress.

Evaluating the raw materials of negotiation

Variables are the raw materials of negotiation. Each one has a scale of possible decisions on which we must settle and agree. For example:

- discount: none or fifty per cent.
- delivery: this afternoon, at exactly 3pm, this week, next week, sometime . . .

There are often many variables; we need a clear idea of what position on the scale is likely to be acceptable to us, and the relative importance of different ones.

> **The more variables there are, and the harder they are to prioritise, the more complex the negotiation becomes.**

The human interactions inherent in the process complicate the negotiation.

Increasing success

If we are not careful, we may look back after a meeting and conclude we lost out. Perhaps we failed to recognise the need for negotiation. If such an underestimate is made, then any transaction will be handled inadequately and the end result is likely to be a bad deal.

Example

For example, an administration manager may telephone a supplier to complain about an incorrectly completed service on a company car. A complaint may produce no more than an apology. If the manager wants something done about it he or she must suggest a remedy: maybe balancing the inconvenience of the car going back in with the seriousness of the fault and the option of leaving it until the next service.

There are many different approaches possible here, and very different arrangements may result from them. If you see something as negotiation, but go at it like 'a bull at a gate', or focus exclusively on one element or allow the transaction to develop into an argument, you are unlikely to achieve what you want.

Knowing the fundamentals of success

Success in negotiation rests on three interrelated fundamentals:

- *What you do*. The techniques and processes of all sorts that are involved.

- *How you go about it*. The manner you employ and the effects this has on those with whom you negotiate.

- *Preparation*. The first two fundamentals are both dependent on this. Given the complexities already mentioned, preparing for negotiation is no more than common sense. Yet it is easier said than done. Probably more negotiators fail to reach the best arrangement for want of adequate preparation than for any other reason. This links to two further important points.

Working at success

It was Vidal Sassoon who said: 'The only place where success comes before work is in the dictionary.' Success in negotiation, as in so much else in life, does not just happen. People with good skills in this area tend to make it look easy. A good cook or a skillful public speaker make what they do seem effortless, but this does not mean that a good deal of preparation has not been necessary for this impression to be given.

Accepting that some preparation is *always* necessary, however long or short the process may need to be, is the first step to success.

Creating an 'edge'

Secondly, and this may compensate if preparation sounds like a bit of a chore, sound preparation can give you your first 'edge' in negotiation. It can act, almost regardless of other factors, to give you a head start in comparison with another person, particularly one who has skimped in this area.

Such an edge is often vital. In many kinds of negotiation no quarter is given. Think of the vehemence of some international negotiations between nations, or of certain wage-bargaining situations. A great deal may hang on the outcome and the negotiator needs to have every trick of the trade on their side in order to create an edge.

The following story takes sales situations as its base and reinforces the need for creating as much of an edge as possible.

It is any buyer's job to get the best possible deal for their organisation. That is what they are paid for; they are not actually on the sales people's side, and will attempt to get the better of them in any way they can, especially with regard to price.

This is well illustrated by the apocryphal story of the fairground strongman. During his act he took an orange, put it in the crook of his arm and, bending his arm, squeezed the juice out. He then challenged anyone in the audience to squeeze out any more, offering a cash prize to anyone who could successfully squeeze out even one more drop.

After many had tried unsuccessfully, one apparently unlikely candidate came forward. He squeezed and squeezed, and finally out came just a couple more drops. The strongman was amazed and, seeking to explain how it was possible, asked as he paid up what the man did for a living. 'I'm a buyer with Ford Motor Company.'

Buyers are not really like this; they are worse.

Source: Adapted from P. Forsyth, *Everything you need to know about marketing* (Kogan Page, 1995).

Such people really are there in part to apply pressure to get the best deal. And it is not just buyers in major companies, or indeed buyers in general, who do this. It could be anyone you negotiate with. They will be intent on fighting their corner, meeting their objectives, financial or otherwise, and will do their best for their position – not yours.

Preparing, and preparing sufficiently thoroughly to influence what you do is well worth while. The next question concerns how to go about it.

PREPARING TO NEGOTIATE

Do you think of yourself as inexperienced at – even wary of – the process of negotiation? This is, at least in part, only because you are ill-prepared for doing it. Being well-prepared breeds confidence. Confidence allows the process to be better managed than an *ad hoc* approach ever will. In addition, appearing confident will be read by others as competence; the way we appear is very important, as we will explore later.

Considering preparation

Preparation may constitute just a few moments' thought prior to the start of a conversation. It may be a few minutes, or an hour or two of homework. Or it may mean sitting round the table with colleagues, thrashing out the best way forward and sometimes even rehearsing what will be done.

Whatever scale of preparation circumstances dictate, it must **always** take place.

RELATING TO OTHERS

Preparation cannot be done in a vacuum. You need to consider

- the other people involved
- your own position.

Considering the other people involved

The first stage of preparation is to consider the person (or people) with whom you must negotiate and, if appropriate, the organisation they represent. Negotiation may take place with all sorts of people: customers, suppliers, business colleagues (boss, subordinates) and you may or may not know them personally.

The questions to ask
Questions need to be answered about such people, for example:

- What role and/or intentions do they have?

- What needs (subjective and objective) do they have?

- What problems will they raise?

- What objections will they raise?

- Can they decide things, or must they consult with someone else?

Each situation will raise different issues, but the principle of thinking through how people may handle something is similar in each case. Do not overlook this, or assume familiarity makes it unnecessary.

Even with people you know and deal with regularly, such analysis may pay dividends.

Example: negotiating with a banquet manager
Suppose you are making arrangements with the banquet manager at a hotel or conference centre for the annual company general meeting. You want it to go well. You want the arrangements to be appropriate. You want it to be memorable. The banquet manager wants it to go well too, of course, but he is also concerned that it should fit in with other functions, be easy to staff and be profitable.

For your part you must be sure the banquet manager has sufficient authority to make the arrangements you want, that he is professional, knowledgeable, and that what he says will be possible proves to be so on the day.

Suppose he suggests a combination of rooms A and B. You feel B and C would suit better. Is his suggestion based on how your group will be best accommodated, or to allow him to fit the local football club in room C? And do you want them next door anyway?

As each element such as cost and catering is discussed and various options reviewed, your knowledge of the banquet manager and his intentions will allow you to negotiate more successfully than if you knew nothing. You may never have met him before, but some consideration of what he is likely to be feeling and planning will always help. This is true of whoever you deal with.

Considering your own position

The other party involved is, of course, yourself. How *you* are seen is important, too. People will respect you more if they feel you appear professional, or expert, if you clearly have the authority to negotiate, if you appear prepared, confident and in charge.

You may never be quite as close to this ideal as you would like, but often the other person has no way of knowing this and 'appear' is indeed the right word. Some people seem to have the confidence to tell you black is white and make you believe it. The exception to this is appearing prepared. You must, as has been said, *actually be* prepared, though it does no harm to appear even better prepared than you actually are. All this means it is essential to think about matters thoroughly.

SETTING OBJECTIVES

Having objectives firmly in mind is key, but surely there is no problem in making them clear? Let us pick up the example of the company annual meeting.

Example: making objectives clear
The objectives for the annual company meeting were effectively stated as being that it should be

- successful
- felt by everyone to be appropriate in style and purpose
- memorable: setting the scene for the year to come.

But there is more. What about cost? Are these objectives regardless of cost or do they have to be achieved within a budget? What about equipment and visual aids? This introduces another area of variables, and another scale against which matters must be judged and settled.

The answer might be that the objectives are certainly not regardless of cost, but that the budget must be realistic if what is wanted is to be achieved well. Similarly, if visual aids are vital, the date of the meeting itself could be changed to secure a larger and better equipped meeting room, where the right equipment can easily be accommodated and a more professional show can be put on.

Setting realistic objectives
You need to identify and set specific (and thus measurable) objectives. You need to have your priorities clear, and clearly related to what variables are involved, and understand your attitude to each. For example, are there some variables about which you are prepared to compromise? If so, how far? And are there others about which you intend to be immovable?

Timing
You may want to consider another key factor: **timing**.

- Are you intent on achieving everything at once, in one meeting?

- Or is there a long term strategy involved?

The reason for thinking through what your objectives are is not academic. It is so that your clarity and surety about them help you conduct the kind of meeting that will help you reach them. 'Ready, aim, fire' is always likely to be the best order in which to proceed!

STRUCTURING THE MEETING

The thinking above is designed to influence the way a meeting works. In fact, your preparation should anticipate something of all the factors that make up the complexities of negotiation (thus we return to it in the last chapter in a summary).

Preparation also includes matters relevant to the message with which the negotiation is bound up. For example, you may need to think how arguments can be justified as your point of view is explained. This goes back to general communication and its focus; for example, making things persuasive.

Using variables as concessions

As we have seen, the variable factors of negotiation are, in effect, traded. You may find the jargon here confusing, as some people use '**variable**' and '**concession**' almost interchangeably. In fact, while all variables may be traded, not all may be used as concessions in the sense of giving something away. But here the only point to make is that you will handle this give-and-take process much better if you have thought through some of the options.

Example: working with variables
Continuing the example of the company annual meeting, the organiser might deal with the banquet manager thus: 'If we start an hour later, and choose an alternative menu, can we have the larger room at the same cost?'

Here three elements; timing, menu and room options, are being used together in relation to overall cost – and within a sentence. Such a discussion can get very much more complicated.

Maintaining structure in the meeting

Structure means the shape and to some extent the style of the meeting. Structure encompasses everything that will avoid any sort of muddle.

* What do you envisage?
* What will you aim to do first, second and third?

Account needs to be taken of likely timing. For example, do you have one hour, several hours, or must everything be agreed more promptly? Your order of sequence and priority must fit within the duration of the meeting. You will need to be very clear which are primary and which are secondary matters. If time runs short you do not want to find you have omitted anything of primary concern.

A well written report has a beginning, a middle and end; so does a good presentation. Both may require a detailed structure within each main segment, however, and a negotiation meeting is similar.

Anticipating the tone of the meeting
As well as *what* you want to do, *how* do you want it to go in terms of manner and feeling?

For example, there may be stages at which you wish to be seen as particularly reasonable, or the opposite, and stages when you need to come over with some real clout.

What kind of personal profile do you wish to project? Make sure that your negotiating style is not in conflict with this. One should enhance the other.

Remaining flexible
While preparation is important, don't cast it in tablets of stone. You can never know for sure what the other party will do, but a clear plan still helps. It sets out your intention: what you would like to do.

Think of your plan like a route map, not a straightjacket. Good planning should not prevent you being flexible and responding to circumstances. Indeed it makes it easier to do so. A route map does not prevent you from changing your route if you unexpectedly find road works in the way. Indeed it helps you both divert and get back on track.

Preparation is the foundation of successful negotiation.

Negotiation does not just happen, nor does the detail of how the meeting needs to progress. As we review the conduct of negotiation, both the shape of the meeting and the detail within that shape will become clearer.

CHECKLIST

1. Negotiation involves more than one party; a win-win approach tends to do best for both.

2. Variables are the raw material of negotiating and success rests to a large extent on how you handle them.

3. If you do not know where you are going it is difficult to proceed with precision; set clear objectives.

4. Prepare carefully, what you will do, how you will do it and take a view of both sides of the situation.

CASE STUDY

Pat seeks a good deal

Pat, a freelance journalist, writes articles, company material and does some public relations work. Working partly from home her business is thriving – so much so that she has decided that the now aging equipment she has at home must give way to a more up-to-date computer and printer.

After some research she has decided on the equipment that will suit her, and has asked a salesman from an office equipment firm to visit her to discuss the quotation he has submitted. Writing in part on business topics, and meeting with many business managers during her work, something about professional techniques has rubbed off on her and she is determined to get a good deal.

Jean needs to be considered

Jean helps Pat on a part-time basis. She will also use any new equipment, and must be able to do so productively and successfully. Being older she is a little wary of what she sees as 'new-fangled stuff', but now deals well with the existing machine. Pat wants to keep her happy and plans to make sure that the change is something she will ultimately approve.

John is confident of a deal

John works for Computer Clobber. He is an experienced salesman. He understands the equipment he sells, is keen to make a sale and knows he must strike a satisfactory deal if he is to get the business. Indeed, from his previous conversation with Pat, he believes that she likes the package of equipment he has recommended; he confidently expects to conclude the deal at the scheduled meeting. He looks forward to receiving his commission.

Pat sees two tasks ahead

She needs to sit down with Jean and discuss the matter. She has three reasons.

1. To make sure that Jean feels involved. If Jean thinks the new equipment is something she helped select, then she is more likely to accept the change.

2. Pat wants to check if Jean can think of anything that may affect the need they have for the equipment and what it can do.

3. She wants to try out some thoughts about her meeting with the salesman. Two heads are better than one.

Pat is sensible enough to realise she must sit down quietly and prepare for the meeting. John does this for a living; she could easily be taken advantage of, but is determined to get a good deal.

Thereafter, with Jean feeling better about the change and with some notes to work from at the meeting, she is ready for the next stage.

DISCUSSION POINTS

1. What variables do your own negotiation meetings involve? Take time to think this through. Are you overlooking any possibilities?

2. How much preparation should you do? What form should this preparation take? Would a colleague acting as a sounding board be useful?

3
Negotiating Tactics

'The height of cleverness is to be able to conceal it.'

Duc de la Rochefoucauld

CONDUCTING THE NEGOTIATION

The complexities of negotiation put a high premium on managing the meeting effectively. During the process two separate factors are in train together:

- the process – the tactics of negotiation, and

- the interpersonal behaviour which accompanies them.

Both are important – separately and as they work together. In order to build up a clear picture of the process, we leave the interpersonal behaviour on one side for the moment and deal specifically with the tactical basis for negotiation.

Using variables: the fundamentals
A knowledge of all the variables, and their possible use in trading, is key.

1. See variables in the round in order to prepare an opening strategy – a starting point for discussion.

2. Decide how the variables can be used to trade. Assess their respective worth.

3. Continue to search throughout the negotiation for other factors that might be used as variables.

Occasionally one party in negotiation holds all the cards and the result may be in little doubt. More often the situation is not a foregone conclusion. The balance might go either way and things start apparently on a flat field, but many arrangements are possible.

Using power in negotiation

What acts to swing the balance? It is the **power** to negotiate that both sides 'bring to the table'. Everyone hopes to have the balance of power. It is something to consider in your planning and certainly something to be realistic about; a major mistake for negotiators is to over- or underestimate the power held either by themselves or by their opposite number.

The word power is used here in a very specific manner. Negotiators mean a number of things by it. The main power factors are as follows.

Using specific variables

The most obvious sources of power are the specific variables that are most important to a particular negotiation. These can be almost anything, from major matters like financial arrangements including price, discounts and payment terms, to a plethora of others.

They can be either tangible or intangible, and usually both are involved. This is an area where feeling is as important as substance. For instance, aspects of the company meeting mentioned earlier may well be subjective: how will the way it is organised affect the participants?

Using a promise of reward

This term describes something you can offer that the other party definitely wants, so they are bound to listen. The banquet manager in the example earlier *wants* the business, giving one major element of power to the organiser. There is a corresponding negative side to this which is identified by the next heading.

Using a threat of punishment

This is where there is an apparent intention *not* to give something that the other party wants. Thus, if the banquet manager refuses to agree some factor important to the organiser, he wields power; this may be increased if the organiser knows it is short notice and he is unlikely to get availability and a better deal elsewhere.

Using legitimacy

Legitimacy means the factual evidence. It can swing the balance without much argument: for example, if the event organiser shows a written quote from another venue then, provided it compares like with like, its presence influences both parties.

Using bogeys

Bogeys are factors used specifically to produce an edge. They may not stand up to great examination, but in the throes of a meeting can be used to good effect. For example, saying 'My chairman is insistent upon . . .' may label a particular point as unalterable – while the truth of the matter may be unclear.

Bogies may be factors used only for what they can achieve, or may be factors that are actually of some importance, but which are given artificial weight in the hopes of their securing an edge.

Showing confidence

Confidence comes in part from preparation. It has a lot to do with the human and behavioural aspects of negotiation, which are explored in depth later. It is harder to deal with someone who appears very confident, and who seems to have every reason to be so. Clearly, you want to feel that the one with the most justifiable confidence is you, and work in every way possible to achieve this.

As you think through what the bargaining variables are, try to assess the power they give you. This is *not* simply a numbers game. Having a larger number of variables, while undeniably useful, may not itself guarantee more negotiating power. Some variables may be lightweight and make little difference; others may be particularly telling and powerful.

Categorising variables

Negotiating variables differ both in nature and potential. Similarly, their roles in trading may vary. Linking them to your plan and objectives will show you their potential role in the subsequent proceedings.

Three types of variable are usually highlighted.

The must haves

Those factors you feel you must take from the negotiation if the deal is to be at all acceptable to you.

The ideals

Those factors which you would like to achieve, and which would constitute the ideal deal. Realistically these must include factors around which you are prepared to make some compromise.

The loss leaders

Loss leaders take their name from products sold in stores at nil or negative profit margins simply to attract in buyers; the buyers then create profit by purchasing other products on their visit. In negotiation we mean those aspects we are really prepared to trade with, even if we would prefer not to, in order to finalise. You must have some things in this category. Trading is fundamental to negotiation. There is, in a way, a ritual to be completed, and without that no progress is possible. If all you do is state an unchangeable position and refuse to move, the outcome may be permanent stalemate.

Some say this was what caused Sir Edward Heath's downfall as Prime Minister years ago; during the miners' strike he did just this. Believing his first offer could not, by definition, be his last the miners dug in their heels. There was effectively no negotiation, and the government toppled.

With a view of what you have to work with in mind we can now turn to the tactical principles that will help you conduct an effective meeting.

FOCUSING ON THE KEY PRINCIPLES

There are four guiding principles which combine to help the successful management of negotiations.

1. Set your sights high.

2. Find out the other person's full intentions.

3. Keep the entirety of the factors in play in mind.

4. Keep looking for further variables.

Setting your sights high
'Faint heart never won fair lady' says an old saying. Always aim high. It is important to aim for the top, for the best deal you can imagine, because it is always easier to manage the process from this starting point. You can always trade down; indeed you may often have to do so, but it is more difficult to trade *up* having stated lower intentions. It is especially difficult to change tactics and trade up well into the meeting.

It is for this reason that having a clear view of the variables – the must haves, etc, detailed above – is so useful. You may not always achieve exactly what you want, but the chances of getting close are most likely with this approach.

Finding out the other person's full intentions

Think of the other person in the same way as you think of yourself. They too have a shopping list of what they want to do. The better your information about what this is, the better you will be able to operate. It is easy to make superficial judgments. There may well be some obvious things they are after, but other factors matter too, as do their priorities. The more complete your picture the better.

Information may come from:

• prior preparation

• knowledge or experience of the person or situation, or ones like them

• questions asked as an integral, perhaps early, part of the negotiation meeting.

Infer sensibly by all means, but be wary of making unwarranted assumptions as this can lead you on false trails if you are wrong. It is all too easy to come out of a meeting that has not gone so well, saying 'but it seemed so obvious . . .'. Your thinking so may have been the other's exact intention.

Keeping all the factors in mind

As the picture builds up, the complexities grow. It is easy as you plan ahead to forget some of the issues you need to keep in mind. You need to keep a clear head, to make notes, think and recap as necessary if each step forward is going to work.

Keeping a look out for further variables

You need to remain flexible. Avoid getting locked in to previous plans; remember planning is only a guide. The good negotiator is quick on their feet. Sometimes what happens is very much along the lines you expect, but some fine tuning is always necessary – and sometimes a great deal needs to be done.

The saying that 'everything is negotiable' can be true. Certainly something that has been described as fixed may suddenly come into play. There is merit in remaining open minded to such possibilities and, where appropriate, taking the initiative.

MANAGING THE PROCESS

The process of negotiation assumes what is called a **point of balance**. It is inherent in the process that while participants start far apart on the scale of possibilities for agreement, they will settle on something they can both relate to as a reasonable deal. (See Figure 5.)

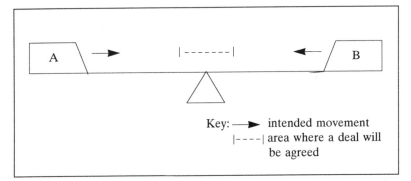

Key: ──▶ intended movement
|----| area where a deal will
be agreed

Fig. 5. The point of balance.

The point of balance on which agreement is struck is not, of course, usually spot on the centre. A range of solutions is possible around the middle point. Similarly the furthest – or most extreme – points from the centre are usually quickly recognised by both parties as unrealistic goals and only relevant as starting points. Movement along the scale is what characterises a discussion as negotiating.

Acknowledging the history of contact

Negotiation rarely comes out of the blue. There is usually a history of contact between the two parties, which may include written contact such as correspondence, or earlier meetings. Whether extensive or minimal such initial communication sets the scene and to some extent provides the agenda.

Negotiation needs an agenda. It may be useful to recap, to refer to the case so far, to any agreements made or indications given, or to whatever history may be useful or necessary. Persuasion proceeds negotiation, so if the first contacts were concerned with a more fundamental agreement, and a case had to be accepted before terms and conditions could be debated, then this too may need to be referred to.

The initial stance

This phrase refers to the **starting point** that each party goes for. Some judgment is necessary in choosing this, as the right starting point can facilitate the moves you want to make thereafter. There are many options.

Going for the quick kill

At one end of the scale you can go for what is described as the quick kill. 'Here are my conditions, take them or leave them.' Such an approach does not, in fact, rule out negotiation. It simply starts by making it clear a hard approach is being taken and little will be given away.

Working from a powerful position, this – or something well to one end – may be an appropriate starting point. It is often used in wage bargaining. But even though it implies strength it must allow for some change or it risks being rejected out of hand. The ritual is important and if people expect some movement this approach may stretch their credibility.

Taking a softer approach

At the other end of the scale, or towards it, the conversation might start on a different note, something like: 'Let's talk about what you want. We are reasonable people and want to secure agreement.'

This may be more suitable when you do not have such a clearly strong case, but go too far with it and it will create, or increase, disadvantage.

It is sometimes said that the higher the opening bid (initial stance), the better the final deal achieved by whoever makes it. Certainly it is difficult to negotiate down from nothing, and an initially exaggerated stance can pull the other party off balance and change their perception about the kind of deal that might be struck. This can mean that the first phase of negotiation is only a clarification of initial stances. A better, less extreme, point is then adopted by each party. Then negotiation *really* gets under way.

Building bridges to agreement

Consider what is going on as the negotiation commences. On the one hand taking initial stances distances participants, like two knights taking up positions on opposite hill tops prior to meeting to do battle in the valley between.

On the other hand, and because of this, there is a need to build **bridges of rapport**. These are inserted to bring the parties together –

or at least closer together – in a way that prompts discussion and sets the scene for what needs to be achieved. Each party will introduce bridges that help their own case.

The other party is more likely to see your point of view if they can relate to your position and circumstance. Bridges make this more likely. There are many approaches, for example:

- Open the discussions on a neutral subject, to allay any hostility, obtain some initial agreement and get the other person talking.

- When holding back, give assurance that you will make every effort to come to a mutually agreeable outcome.

- Demonstrate respect for both the other party and the process you are embarking on. For example, compliment them about something already done that helps the process.

- Refer back to past agreement. This reinforces persuasion.

- Present some of the values in your offering, even if you plan to negotiate them out later.

- Be clear about complex issues.

All such tactics put the conversation on a basis of sweet reason. Even attempts to get the other party's list of requirements on the table can be undertaken in a way that seems helpful: take an interest in them, their needs and views. This combines a show of genuine concern with something that, in fact, strengthens your position.

Keeping finding out
Ask questions, and listen – really listen – to the answers. Get the other parties' position clearly in mind. Information is power in negotiation, and while you do not want to make people feel they are undergoing the Spanish Inquisition, the more you discover the better. Try to strike the right balance.

Starting to trade early on
Trading concessions may well start at this stage. Even if they initially reflect peripheral issues, it can still set the scene for what follows. Avoid giving anything away early on. Even saying, 'Why don't we talk this through over lunch – my treat', may give the wrong impression.

Better to say, 'If you agree to come to an agreement today, then I will buy us lunch and we can chat this through in comfort.' If this kind of swap is handled informally, then no one need feel boxed in. The conversation can move naturally to a more business-like level. Then the trading can really start.

Trading concessions: the rules
Trading can take the form of tentative exploration, as in the example above on a 'if ... then ...' basis. Alternatively, it may take on a more demanding tone. In either case two important overall rules apply at this stage.

Rule 1: never give a concession – trade it reluctantly
The first part ('never give') is important because the number of variables is finite and you want your share. The second is, too, because perception is as important to how things go as fact. You want to be seen to be driving a hard bargain, otherwise you may not be taken seriously.

Rule 2: optimise or minimise every concession
This means optimising your concessions and minimising theirs. You can do this in terms of both value and how you talk about them. Try to build up the value, significance and importance of anything you offer and minimise that of what is offered to you.

The two sides of this process are worth exploring.

Optimising your concessions
This means:

- Stressing the cost (financial or otherwise) to you: 'Well, I could do that but it will involve me in a lot more work'.

- Exaggerating, but maintaining credibility. Do not overstate and, if possible, provide evidence. 'Well, I could do that but it will involve me in at least twice as much work. I have just been through ...'.

- Referring to a major problem which your concession will solve. 'I suppose, if I was to agree that, it would remove the need for you to ...'.

- Implying that you are making an exceptional concession. 'I would never normally do this, but ...'.

Another approach, suitable for someone you have met before is:

- Referring to past discussions, and their successful outcome, and what you did for them. 'Remember how useful so and so was? I suppose we could go that route again, how about . . .'.

Such lead-ins not only build the significance of what you are offering, and make it more acceptable, but also make it more likely to be accepted quickly because there is an implied urgency. This is something that you may elect to exaggerate where appropriate.

Minimising their concessions
Even if you plan to accept the concessions this means:

- Not overdoing the thanks. Not a profuse 'Thank you so much', but a brief, even dismissive 'thanks'. This is as much a matter of tone as of the words used.

- Depreciating them, belittling the value: 'Right, that's a small step forward, I guess'.

- Amortising them where appropriate. That is, divide them where smaller units will sound less impressive. 'Well, at least that would save me X every month', rather than quoting the annual figure.

- Treating them as given and thus of no real value. A brief acknowledgement may be all that is necessary to give this impression: 'Right, let's do it that way'.

- Taking it for granted, in fact saying it is not a concession at all but a foregone conclusion: 'Fine, I was certainly assuming that . . .'.

- Devaluing by implying you already have what is being offered; 'OK, though I already have . . .'.

- Accepting, but in doing so implying that you are doing a favour: 'I don't really need that, but fine, let's arrange things that way if it helps'.

- Linking value to time, implying it is now not worth what is implied: 'Well, that helps a little, but it isn't of major importance now we have . . .'.

– Denying any value: 'That really doesn't help'.

Minimising concessions does not work in every environment. In the Middle East the reverse is necessary. Always check local conditions if you have to work overseas.

Creating a trading edge

As concessions are either minimised or optimised as appropriate, the skilled negotiator trades a concession which in fact costs them little. It has, though, an *implied* value which brings a relatively *more* valuable concession in return from the other side.

It is this difference in value that gives an edge. A concession which you offer, but imply is of little or no value, is likely to prompt the offer of a low value concession in return. Thus throughout the process you must play down your thanks for concessions gained and imply their low value, and build up the value of everything that you may concede. The only restraint on this exaggeration is the need to retain credibility with the other person.

It is all a question of degree. People know there is a ritual to negotiation, but still have to form a judgment of how far this goes.

KEEPING ON TRACK

There can be a large number of balls in the air during negotiation. Keeping track of the variables is quite a task, but you can prepare for it. If you have thought through what you want to do, considered the possibilities and anticipated the reaction of the other side, then you will have a picture that you can amend and adapt as discussions proceed. It may help to imagine the variables as boxes of different weights.

The dangers here are very real. If you forget something, or don't deal with it appropriately and at the right time, it may be impossible to bring it up later, or from a strong position. Make sure you have the overall position clearly in mind as you deal with the various points. If *you* are organised then anyone less so is at a disadvantage in dealing with you, so this can produce another edge.

USING TECHNIQUES TO KEEP AHEAD

With the above rules in mind we will conclude this chapter by reviewing some other techniques to make your negotiating work effectively. These ten key ideas are basic but useful techniques and begin to demonstrate the process at work.

1. Using silence

Saying nothing can sometimes be as powerful as speaking, providing silence is used at the right time and in the right way. As most people quickly feel embarrassed by a silence, after even a few seconds, it can need a conscious effort to hold it, but it can be worthwhile.

- In trading concessions, if you cannot optimise or minimise, silence can imply that you are non-committal.

- Being silent can imply certainty on your part, and thus uncertainty in another. Having made a clear suggestion – you wait. You will find it's not so difficult to ensure the other person speaks first. Maybe they need to think about it. If you chip in prematurely you may find yourself diluting your case unnecessarily.

Example: using silence

A company buyer was speaking on the telephone to a potential supplier and, with a good quote in front of him, challenging the price without really saying anything clearly: 'I am still a bit concerned about the price'. The supplier defended the deal as being good, which it was. He asked if it did not seem reasonable to the buyer, who said nothing at all. Embarrassed, the supplier started to justify the figures and again ended with a question that was ignored.

After three silences which the supplier found awkward, he said: 'Would another five per cent get the order?'

A silence can be powerful, and if it is not coped with well by the other party is an easy technique with which to win points.

2. Summarising frequently

By definition, negotiations can often be complex. They involve juggling a number of variables. It is easy to lose the thread. Never be afraid to summarise – recap where you have got to so far, how one aspect of the discussion has been left. Linking this to using 'suppose' or 'if' keeps the conversation organised and allows you to explore possibilities without committing yourself until you are ready. You might make this sort of comment: 'Right, we have agreed that we need to sort cost, delivery and timing. Now if we take . . ., then . . .'.

3. Making notes

This too helps keep complex negotiations on track. While certain meetings are too informal for a full note-taking to be appropriate, even a few words noted down can help.

Information is power.

Never leave your self groping for what was said. Not only will the lack of recall worry you, but the fact that you are needing to ask calls your expertise into question and may spur the other party on to try harder.

Not only will taking notes prevent you being caught out over something factual, but making them or checking them can have another advantage. It gives you time to think. As you say: 'Let me just note that down, or as you check: 'Let me just see what we agreed about that,' you can be thinking. The brain works faster than the pen. It is surprising how much thinking you can do as you write two or three (sometimes irrelevant!) words on your pad.

4. Leaving people feeling each step is good
Negotiation typically builds agreement progressively. Make sure you emphasise that each stage is good – preferably for both parties, but particularly for the other party – as you proceed. Phrases like 'that's a good arrangement', 'that will work well', 'that's fair'. 'that's a good suggestion', help build the agreement.

5. Reading between the lines
Remember that negotiation is essentially an adversarial process. Both parties want the best for themselves, and the only signs of any approaching traps come via the other person, as do signs of success round the corner. Watch particularly for danger phrases that often mean something other than they seem to, even the very opposite. For example:

- 'You're a reasonable fellow.' Meaning: 'I am'.

- 'That's much fairer for both of us.' Meaning: 'Especially for me'.

- 'It looks like we are about there.' Meaning: 'There is something else I want'.

- 'All that's left is to sort out a couple of minor details.' Minor? For whom?

- 'That's all, then.' Followed by: 'But there is just one more thing . . .'.

We return to this concept later.

6. Remaining neutral

Maintain neutrality as much and as long as possible. Negotiation works best as a balancing exercise. If you throw the whole basis of discussion up in the air – 'It is not as good as the other deal I am considering' – you risk taking everything back to square one. You may *want* to go back if you are not happy with the offer or the terms and conditions. But if you do you risk returning to another process, that of persuasive communication.

7. Concentrating – all the time

Concentrate. Build in time to think if necessary. The power of silence has been mentioned; use it to think ahead. Use *any* delaying tactic to stop you getting into difficulty, and always engage the brain before the mouth. Use a calculator, make a telephone call or just say 'Let me think about that for a moment', but give yourself pause for thought.

On the other hand, if you can make the other party leap before they look, so much the better.

8. Keeping your powder dry

Beware of acting precipitately. Try not to make an offer, certainly not a final offer, until everything that needs negotiating is on the table. This may need no more than a question: 'Yes, I am sure I can help there, but is there anything else you want to consider?' You may need to probe to be sure of your ground before you proceed.

9. Beware deadlines

It is said that there has not been a deadline in history that was not negotiable. Timing is a variable. How long will things take? When will they happen? All at once? Keep this in mind at all stages of the process.

10. Remembering constraints and variables are interchangeable

Almost anything the other side presents as fixed may be made into a variable. The word fixed is as likely to mean we do not *want* to negotiate this, as it *cannot* be used as a variable. It pays to act accordingly.

Using the techniques
None of these points is, in itself, complex. They illustrate the multi-faceted nature of negotiation, where a great deal is going on. Such techniques are useful; but none is a cure-all that will alone ensure the deal you want. The trick is in the overall orchestration of what you do.

Being in charge
Because of the need to orchestrate a complex process, it helps if you are in the driving seat. A line in Shakespeare's *Much Ado About Nothing* puts it well: 'Two men ride of a horse, one must ride behind'. Meetings, too, need someone in front. Taking a leading role does not have to mean it is a heavy one, indeed it may not even be obvious where direction originates.

> **Run the conversation *you* want, in a way that *they* find they like, or at least find acceptable or professional.**

Getting off to a good start sets the process in train. Fine-tuning as you go along keeps you progressing matters as you want. This means being extra conscious of what the other person appears to be up to, and of how the interpersonal behaviour of the transaction is likely to work.

CHECKLIST

1. Be sure you know what gives you (and them) power.

2. Keep the process manageable: focus on the key operational process of negotiation, such as setting sights high.

3. Plan to make a good start.

4. Deal effectively with the trading that forms the core of negotiation.

5. Know the techniques, and when and how to use them.

CASE STUDY

Negotiating a complex matter

Linda and Harry are due to meet a surveyor, Sue, of the local Council. They need planning permission before they can expand their current site and implement expansion plans for their business.

The matter is complex. There are matters of access, parking and congestion, employment and building regulation. They envisage a long discussion.

Linda and Harry discuss the matter and lay out a strategy. Because of the complexity, they arrange a logical order for the discussion and consider how to persuade Sue to accept it. They divide their task between the two of them; one will lead on some points, another on others. This is primarily to keep things manageable. Though it is important for both to be involved in the discussion, Linda has a smaller load.

One of her tasks is to keep a note of the balance. She will be the note-taker. Having the best view of how things stand at any particular moment, she will be responsible for keeping the two of them on track during discussions, which will inevitably get more confusing as they progress.

Learning from example

The thinking described above makes good sense. Maintaining a vision of the broad picture as you proceed is as important as the tactics deployed at a particular moment to settle an issue.

Note that when more than one person on each side is involved in discussions, how the team organises itself becomes a variable and a key factor in securing an edge. In good teamwork one and one makes *more* than two. It should appear seamless, and can add considerable strength to a situation if it is deployed as an active ingredient and made to work well.

DISCUSSION POINTS

1. What techniques can you use appropriately and with confidence?

2. What techniques do you need to experiment and practice with?

3. What mix of methodology best suits your situation and the kind of people with whom you must negotiate?

4
Getting Under Way

'Nothing ever becomes real until it is experienced – even a proverb is no proverb to you till your life has illustrated it.'

John Keats

LINKING THEORY AND PRACTICE

Enough has been said to demonstrate that negotiation is a practical art. It is one thing to dissect and discuss it, but it is another to put it into practice. We will examine in more detail the case introduced in Chapter 2, to look at the principles knit together in reality.

Case study

The case study illustrates a simple commercial situation. The process would be essentially similar to a non-commercial environment where any two people must negotiate. In this conversation the decision to purchase has been made, *provided* Pat can get the sort of deal she wants. If not she would be prepared to talk to another supplier. Below is what each protagonist plans to get from the meeting.

Pat wants to keep costs down
Pat has debated long and hard with herself about what she can afford. It is very important to her to have something good. She wants the larger and faster of the two printers she has checked out. Above all she would like to minimise the cost. Yet by going into the matter she has realised there are additional items such as extra software that could be worth obtaining as well. The specifications in the quote include two additional software packages.

Finally, a small point. She is worried about being away from her desk for any training that may be necessary.

John is confident of a sale
John believes he is close to an order. The equipment seems to be exactly what is wanted and he has offered a reasonable deal. He has

some leeway on price, either in terms of a reduction or juggling with other elements of the package, but wants a profitable sale. He sees it as the last part of the sales process rather than a negotiation. He is mistaken in this view and therefore not as appropriately prepared as he should be.

Looking out for variables
Various elements are used as variables during the conversation. These include: the equipment itself, the software, delivery and installation, training, payment terms, price and discount and even publicity.
Note: Comments appear in italics periodically about the conversation as it proceeds. There are numbers marking various stages; these link to a checklist later in the chapter.

MANAGING THE EBB AND FLOW OF THE PROCESS

John (J) is sitting in Pat's (P) office. The initial pleasantries are over, Sue has organised them coffee, and John now takes the initiative and turns to the business of the day.

J You got our quote then?

P Yes, thanks very much.

He tests to discover her initial attitude.

J I hope you found it interesting.

P Yes, indeed. I am not sure it is exactly right and I am comparing it with some others, but it was certainly clear. (1)

She indicates that she is looking at other quotes and hints they are also good, perhaps better.

J I see, in what way is ours not quite right?

He attempts to clarify her last remark.

P Technically I am sure it is quite good. I am not a technical person (2), of course, but you seem to have reflected my brief well enough and I have no quibbles with that. However, I am after a total system. Not just the word

She begins to soften up John.

processor itself, but the software, printer and things like training as well. I think it's these areas we need to have a closer look at.

J I see, perhaps you would tell me where you see any particular problem?

He seeks further clarification.

P I think there are several areas. Perhaps we can take them one at a time. Let's deal with the ancillary equipment first. In your quote you recommend the faster of the two laser printers we discussed. As you know I really want the faster printer rather than the more basic one if I can, and both a $3^1/_2$ inch disk drive and a CD-ROM, so I can liaise with a colleague who has material on that system and get myself more up-to-date.

P prefers to deal with one thing at a time and in the sequence of her choice. She starts with the other equipment.

Now this will certainly do everything I want – a Rolls Royce job in fact – but that printer does make the whole package more than I really hoped to spend (3). I am not sure that the second disk drive is essential anyway. I am well able to manage without it. So what I suggest we do is that you let me have the CD-ROM drive on loan long enough to test it out.

P indicates the total is too expensive.

P asks for a concession, trading something of low importance to her: the two drives.

J It is just the additional disk drive that you want on that basis?

J clarifies.

P Yes. If I do want to keep it

This was always her intention.

then it will postpone the payment for that element for just a while and that means I can go for the better printer. See what I mean?

J Yes, I do.

P It won't be difficult for you to arrange that (4) I am sure, and if I decide in favour you will get payment for it anyway in, say, six months.

P minimises the difficulty the point may make for him.

J Okay, I suppose I can arrange that. I'm pretty sure you will want to keep it anyway.

J concedes what appears a small point.

P I expect you're right. Good, that's fine. Let's turn now to the question of software. I would ideally like the graphics package, and the one that will do my accounts as well as the full word processing one. Would you be able to include those at no extra charge? They are not very costly but I must keep the overall cost down, as I've said.

P confirms the concession and turns to the second point: software . . .

. . . and asks for a concession.

J You didn't include those in the spec we quoted, or did you?

J begins to resist.

P No, I'm sorry. I hadn't been through all the literature at the time, but I can see they would be useful. It would make your overall arrangements much more attractive. (5)

P apologises and repeats the request.

J It is an extra cost for us, though.

J continues to resist.

P Not very much in terms of the

P persists, minimising the effect.

overall cost.

J Well, perhaps not. I guess I could let you have those if we go ahead.

J agrees, reluctantly, to include the extra software.

P And you will deliver that along with everything else and include a run-down on them in the training?

P adds on a request for a small, associated, concession.

J Well I don't know, it will extend the training time and . . .

J realises he has in fact given away more than he thought.

P But they are not much good unless I can work them. I am sure I will pick it up fast and it won't extend the time to any real extent.

The point is pressed and the difficulty (time and cost) minimised.

J All right.

He agrees.

P I appreciate that. Now, what next? Ah yes, the delivery and installation.

P raises the third point: delivery and installation.

J Well, that should be straightforward. Is that the last point?

J attempts to get the rest of her shopping list.

P Yes. (6) Well, apart from training but I am sure that's no problem. It's all included and you agreed to run me through the other software.

P belittles what is described as the last point.

J Yes, okay. What about delivery? Here I suppose?

Reassured, J goes back to the third point.

P That's right. I've ordered one of those units for it all to stand. Once I know which quote I accept I can get that and away we go. Your people do install, don't they? I don't want a pile of boxes dumped on the doorstep.

J Yes, of course. Delivery and installation were all included.

P And you will take away all the boxes and packing?

P asks for a small extra.

J We don't usually do that. Can't you leave them for the dustman?

J resists.

P The residents' association is a bit strict about that sort of thing and the chairman lives next door. In fact, he wants to come and see what equipment I get. If you can get all the boxes taken away I can possibly recommend you. (7) I believe he is thinking of a similar installation for his firm.

P hints at future business prospects as a lever to obtain the concession.

J I'm still not sure that I can arrange that. Our despatch manager is very strict.

P See what you can do, will you?

This point is left hanging but P has a nice case to make to whoever delivers: 'He said he'd fix it'.

J Okay, I will. Now what about training? If you decide to go ahead today, then I can get a date in the diary for you to visit the training centre.

J tries to move on to the last point and explains what needs to be done.

P And you think a day will be enough – even with the other software included?

P checks details.

J Oh yes, certainly. How about the week after next?

J goes for agreement.

P Hang on, I was hoping you could get your trainer to come here. Would that be possible?

P introduces another, expected, concession she requires.

J It is certainly possible, but

J is determined to give nothing

there would be an extra cost. *away.*

P You remember I mentioned earlier the other quotes I have? (8)

J Yes.

J One of the differences is that they are both willing to do the training here. It means I don't have to leave my phone unattended. That's important to someone working on their own. If we schedule the date well ahead it would minimise the inconvenience.

P makes him feel uncompetitive, just at a stage when he believes everything is agreed, and minimises the problem.

J Even so, we have a clear scale of charges for in-house visits and with what I have already agreed . . .

J resists.

P I see the problem but it would be a pity to fall out at this stage. Everything else seems fine. May I make a suggestion?

P emphasises the prospect of the order.

J What, exactly?

J tries to clarify.

P I have been asked by one of the office equipment journals (she names a well known one) to write a feature on the writer's use of word processors. If I buy yours I shall have to use it as an example – after all it will be the only one I've got! If I promise to mention your firm by name, do you think your boss would agree to the training being done here? It would be such a help. At least ask him, he might like the idea. (9)

P makes the request seem to have clear compensations. She sells it.

J I can certainly ask, it sounds a

J conditionally agrees.

good swap to me. Will you leave it with me?

P Yes, of course. See what reaction you get.

J Right. So we seem to be agreed. We let you have the second drive on six months' loan, include the additional software, and I will work on the training being done here.

P And on getting all the boxes cleared away – yes?

J That's right, nearly forgot. Can we go ahead on that basis?

J tries to wrap up the deal.

P Yes, I think we can ... but there is just one small thing. Again this is included in the other quotes. That's insurance.

P raises an extra area.

J What do you mean?

J queries.

P They offer a free year's insurance as part of the package.

J On the same machine and costing?

P Not exactly, I suppose, but similar.

P concedes it is not like for like.

J You have to look at the other deal, you know. With the price we have quoted and the extras there is no possibility of my matching that.

J refuses.

P Well, I suppose I have to accept that. Even so it is a bit of a disappointment. Your company offers the best arrangements in many ways, but even with the items we have agreed it is still not the

P suggests how reasonable she is ...
... raises a price objection

most competitive. I take it you do want the business?

J Yes, indeed we do.

P Perhaps you would consider adjusting the overall discount to make up for my having to fix and pay for insurance separately?

... and makes a suggestion.

J I believe our original price was very keen. We do, as I said, want the order, but I don't really have any more leeway over the discount.

J resists.

P I'm sure your price is keen, but as I said it is not the most competitive.

P puts his quote on the spot by reminding him of the competitors.

J What sort of difference are we talking about?

P To really make everything we have said add up to the best deal all round, I suppose the discount would need to go up by seven and a half per cent or so.

J That's a lot of money, the margins on this kind of system are not so great.

J resists.

P How far could you go?

P squeezes.

J Myself? I think with what we have already agreed I could not go beyond four per cent at this stage. That would be my limit.

P And how far could your company go at the next stage? (10)

P presses to test that the overall limit is really being reached.

J 'At this stage' was just a turn of phrase. Four per cent would be the company's limit.

P No good me calling your boss, you mean?

P questions J's status and authority.

J No, I'm afraid not.

P But you can go to four per cent more discount?

J Yes, I can.

P I hoped you would go to seven and a half per cent to match the others completely, but let's see what we have agreed. You will lend me the second drive and invoice after six months at the current price, you will include the other software and find out about the training – and the boxes – and reduce the price by another four per cent.

P belittles the offer.

P re-caps and throws in the current price.

J Yes, that's it.

P On that basis, I think we have a deal. Would you like another coffee while we tie up the paperwork?

P closes the discussion and the deal.

USING THE DYNAMICS OF THE MEETING

Pat had thought about what she wanted. She had considered the process that was to be involved. She did not expect the meeting to go exactly as planned, but used the changing circumstances to feel her way through it. She had firm objectives, but had to deal with a dynamic situation as the other party, of course, had their own intentions.

There are still loose ends but the deal has improved markedly. It may be that Pat is depicted as doing too well, though no doubt the salesman has still got a profitable deal. She handled it well and deserved to win the majority of points. She certainly did better than others, approaching the same process less well prepared, might have done. We might imagine she did better than John expected, he perhaps departed the meeting muttering about 'customers getting more demanding by the day'.

Adding up the score

The outcome might be summarised as follows. John gets his order, of course, but Pat wins a number of concessions:

– Six months' loan of the CD-ROM disk drive, and later payment for it at current prices.

– Two additional, free, pieces of software.

– The boxes and packing taken away on delivery – perhaps.

– Training at her home, rather than at the training centre – probably. She could have opted to make her order conditional on this.

– An additional four per cent discount.

She has not managed to get free insurance, and has offered collaboration on an article, and tacitly promised a recommendation to a friend.

Pat has saved enough to finance the printer she really wanted and still come out ahead. She led the process: she worked through systematically, she was prepared, she negotiated. John, on the other hand, emerges sadder but wiser. He has the order, it may even be reasonably profitable, but he is no doubt saying to himself 'if only . . .'.

READING THE SIGNS

All negotiation will have a sub-text of hidden meaning. Some words disguise the true feeling, some can draw attention to the fact that all is not quite as it seems.

The numbers in the preceding text indicate some examples of this, and below are related to possible meanings.

Text number	Possible meaning
1. . . . it was certainly clear.	*But not exactly right.*
2. I am not a technical person . . .	*You can handle me easily.*

3. ...does make the whole package more than I really hoped to spend...   *I may not buy unless I get a better deal.*

4. It won't be difficult for you...   *A little flattery...*

5. ...make your overall arrangement much more attractive.   *Without it, it is less or not at all attractive.*

6. Yes.   *For the moment.*

7. ...I can possibly...   *Nothing promised, no degree of likelihood.*

8. Remember ... the other quotes.   *I am not decided yet, don't lose it at this stage.*

9. He might like the idea.   *And thank you for it.*

10. ...at the next stage.   *Can anyone else in your organisation decide differently?*

FINE-TUNING YOUR APPROACH

It is from the thinking done prior to the meeting and the plan made that the first direction springs. As the case here shows, negotiating is a dynamic affair. You can never be sure of what will happen. Even quite minor variances from what is expected or planned can necessitate changes to how the meeting is then handled.

Such changes produce opportunities and challenges. The good negotiator is quick on their feet and remains open to fine-tuning the approach as the meeting proceeds. It is best to assume this will be necessary. You will not anticipate everything, nor will you spot every opportunity, but your opponent will not either. If you can fine-tune in a way that stays a jump ahead, that may be sufficient to get the deal you want.

CHECKLIST

1. Always have a plan and a clear idea of how you intend to deal with the discussion.

2. Resolve to lead whenever possible, though you may not want this to be apparent.

3. Fine-tune as you go to bypass difficulties and take advantage of any opportunity that appears unexpectedly along the way.

DISCUSSION POINTS

1. How can you organise your thinking to help keep you on track?

2. How can you ensure your plan does not act as a straightjacket, but allows for flexibility?

3. What traps are likely to be strewn in your path during the discussions?

5
Refining Your Skills

'I never observe rules of conduct, and therefore have given up making them.'

George Bernard Shaw

USING INTERPERSONAL BEHAVIOUR

Negotiation is not simply a matter of techniques, though these are important. It also depends on reading the behaviour of the other people involved, and using behavioural factors yourself. Reading between the lines and acting accordingly is part of the negotiating ritual. To a degree this is a matter of experience, which needs time to accumulate. Nevertheless certain principles can be useful.

This section looks at key behavioural aspects aspects:

- reading between the lines
- listening
- questioning
- non-verbal signals (body language).

USING VERBAL SIGNS

Negotiation has a language of its own. Some of it becomes ritual, adding nothing to persuasiveness and clearly part of the fabric rather than the content of what is being said. Some is a ploy, and we need to read between the lines to see what motivation lies behind the comment or phrase.

For instance, consider the hidden signals in the following examples:

One party says...	... and means
We would find it extremely difficult to meet the deadline.	If we do meet it, it must be worth something.
Our organisation is not set up to cope with that.	So, if we do, consider it a real favour.
I do not have the authority to arrange...	... but someone else does.
It is not our normal practice to do that.	I could make an exception.
I never negotiate on price.	If you want to – you start.
We can discuss that point.	It is negotiable.
We are not prepared to discuss that at this stage.	But we will later.
That's very much more than our budget.	So it had better offer real value and extra benefit.
It is not our policy to give additional discounts and if we did they would not be as much as ten per cent.	Would you accept five per cent?
Our price for that quantity is X.	But for larger quantities...
That's the standard terms and conditions.	But we could negotiate.
It seems an extremely reasonable arrangement.	It is best for me.
It is a good price.	It is profitable, for us.
I can't say I am happy with the arrangement but...	I agree, but may ask for something else.

You will no doubt spot, or use in future, many more. The detail, the nuances of everything said when negotiating is very important. Does it mean what it seems? Can we check? Is it a ploy? Is it an opportunity? How can we gain an edge with a word or phrase?

It is wise to be constantly watchful, to take nothing at face value. Remember that when you use phrases with nuances they help you; if the other party uses them they may be warning signs, and potentially put you at a disadvantage. Recognising them, and their potential danger, is the first step to overcoming them if they are deployed against you.

USING BEHAVIOURAL TECHNIQUES

Keeping the temperature under control

You negotiate best with a calm, considered approach. So does the other person. Whilst you do not want to make it easy for them, you do not want the fabric of negotiation to collapse either. Any behaviour you use must help your cause without demolishing the process.

It is easy to get into a position where pursuing your cause does more harm than good. For instance, if you labour an issue on which agreement is difficult and refuse to budge, particularly early in a discussion, you may create an impasse from which it is difficult for either party to retreat. You need to keep the range of issues in mind. If necessary leave a point on one side to return to later. Having agreed some of the issues, overall views change. With a deal now in prospect the early sticking point may not seem so important and can be dealt with without real difficulty.

Using hidden motives

Icebergs are a danger to shipping not so much because of what can be seen of them, but because of what can not. The iceberg concept can apply to discussion and negotiation. You ask something and do not seem to get a straight answer. The other party's suspicion may prevent it; they are so busy looking for hidden motives that they hinder agreement for no good reason.

It makes sense to spell out why you are doing things, asking a certain question, pursuing a certain line so that at least most of what is hidden becomes clear. Of course, you may have motives you want hidden, at least for the moment, but it will not help if the other person thinks you are being several times more devious than you are.

Flagging

Clear flagging, or signposting, of how you are proceeding can help. Sometimes it just makes clear what you are doing: 'May I ask ... ?' or 'Perhaps I might suggest ... ?' At other times a specific reason makes getting what we want more likely: 'I think it might be easier to settle other details if we can agree a fixed budget first.' It is seen as a constructive step forward.

On the other hand we should *never* flag disagreement. This is something to watch, as the natural response is to flag it instantly. Consider what happens in a simple example.

Example: encouraging constructive listening
A makes a suggestion: 'Perhaps we can aim for completion of stage one by Friday week'. B immediately disagrees: 'No, I think that's far too long'. Even if he goes on to explain why, and even if he is right, A is busy developing a retaliatory response from the moment he hears the word no. He does not listen to the explanation of why, and even if he half hears it, is already committed to his riposte.

> **People are more likely to listen constructively, and accept reasons, if they are given *before* disagreement is flagged**.

Thus, if A makes his point B might respond: 'That would be ideal. However, we agreed that the whole project should be finished by the end of the month. Does Friday week leave sufficient time for everything else?' There is much more chance that this will prompt thought and discussion, that a compromise can be found or a counter-suggestion accepted.

Summarising progress
Good negotiators summarise regularly; many negotiations get complex and discussions can last a while. Summarising can:

- Test progress and allow you to rephrase things said by the other party.

- Help you gain the initiative in the discussion, or maintain the dialogue.

- Ensure that both parties have similar interpretations of what is said, and thus avoid misunderstanding and subsequent acrimony.

Attacking psychologically
Some things are said not as part of any argument but to put the other party at a psychological disadvantage: – to rattle them. Some may be based on issues which are part of the discussion, such as pressure on timing and deadlines. Others may be solely cosmetic, like the elaborate lighting of a pipe or a pause to make an urgent telephone call,

to create a long silence or pause, during which they are thinking and you are sweating. All sorts of things can be used in this way, amongst them:

- playing for time: working something out on a calculator or making a phone call

- a smoke screen of demands, only one of which is important

- flattery or coercion

- an angry outburst or show of emotion

- apparent total fluency with the facts: wondrous mental arithmetic may have been worked out beforehand, or just be a guess which is said with sufficient authority to sound authoritative

- physical arrangements: an uncomfortable chair or position, balancing a coffee cup and trying to take notes

- financial restraints made to seem irreversible

- pretended misunderstanding.

Avoiding defend/attack spirals

Because people feel it is not proper to hit someone without warning, disagreement often starts from mild beginnings. Whilst one party says 'I am not sure about this', or 'I think we should aim for better than that', gently moving towards a major negative, the other senses what is happening and begins to prepare a counter-argument.

Good negotiators do not put the other party on their guard, and effectively provide time for them to react well. If it is appropriate to attack then they do so without warning.

Proposing counter suggestions

Suppose you make proposal X and then the other person makes proposal Y. If you automatically think they are disagreeing, you will not be receptive and may not consider the alternative properly. If so your riposte can lead into a series of monologues, with both sides seeing the other as unhelpful and unconstructive. Progress is blocked when proposal X and Y are not really so far apart, and things could be moving together. This needs careful judgement.

Avoiding deadlock

The purpose of negotiation is to make a deal. Deadlock does nothing for either party. The search for variables has to go on until a deal is possible. It is usually only a question of time. However, if there are moments of deadlock it is helpful to think of the conversation flowing like a stream, which will always find a path *round* obstructions rather than through them.

Never underestimate the chances of a new path, nor over-estimate your opponent's power and determination to remain unmoving. Try to find out *why* there is deadlock, and search widely for concessions or variables that will break it. In dire cases suggest a break, agreeing as much as possible before it, or even the involvement of other people. Try anything to create a real shift in what is happening.

Using ritual approaches

In certain parts of the world it is necessary to bargain in the shops and markets, not simply to secure a good price but to win respect. The process itself is important, not just the outcome.

This is true of any negotiating situation. Some professional negotiators, who enjoy the game, feel frustrated if agreement is too quick or too simple. Negotiation must be allowed to take its course, and they will put up more and more conditions or elements to keep the process going. In such circumstances it may be wise never to make the first offer, not to make unacceptable conditions or drive impossible bargains.

Example: remembering tradition

A man visiting Hong Kong for the first time wishes to buy a watch. He had been told about the bargaining, and the percentage drop in price for which he should aim. He set off round the shops and, despite his best efforts, could get only half-way towards the suggested discount. Back at the hotel, discussing this with a local colleague, he asked what was he doing wrong. 'How long were you in each shop?' asked the colleague. On hearing that it was ten minutes or so, he suggested the visitor try again and give it half an hour.

The newcomer then discovered that only after twenty minutes or so, when you were sitting on a stool and coffee had been produced, did the bargaining get serious. Next time he came out with a nice watch and a good deal, and a little more understanding about the psychology of negotiation.

There are limits of course, but if the other party wants to take their time, let them. It may be worth it in the end. Timing is an important factor, and has to be handled just right.

Linking to future relationships

Always aim to end on a pleasant note. Negotiation can get acrimonious, hard bargains are driven, but people need to work or play together again. It may be good for future relations for the last move to be towards the other party, maybe throwing in one last small sweetener as the final agreement is made. This can stand you in good stead next time round. With colleagues these may be a regular part of your work.

LISTENING

Many problems of communication are due to people not listening. It is always important, especially in a complex interaction such as negotiation. It is easy to be distracted, and you need to concentrate. Daydreaming, however constructively, is all too easy. Give the other party your undivided attention.

Another distraction is emotion. As the other person's argument unfolds you perhaps begin to feel anxious, or become angry. If such resentment takes over and prevents you listening your case will suffer.

You may want to keep your first reactions hidden. It can be difficult to refer back, saying that something is a minor difficulty if when it was raised your face registered total dismay.

Checking you have listened correctly

Never be afraid to interrupt a long speech to double-check you are following it. Ask for simplification or repetition if you wish. Beware too of hearing what you *want* to hear. Do not make assumptions, act on what the true message is.

You may need to analyse the message as it proceeds and begin to form a response, but you have to keep listening as you do so if you are not to run into problems.

Making listening easier

Finally, think about what will make listening easier. You cannot concentrate on what is being said if there is a lot of background noise, for example, an open-plan office, or if you are busy with something else as you talk, like driving a car. Try to pick a time when you are at your best, not over-tired or distracted by some personal emergency.

> **If you pick up one hundred per cent of the message, you are
> in a much better position to respond effectively.**

QUESTIONING

Always ask sufficient questions to help you with the whole process.
Ask about the other person, their situation, their needs, their priorities. Open questions, those which cannot be answered simply yes or
no and tend to start with what, where, why, how, who, are usually best.
They get people talking and produce more information. This is the
raw material for your case.

It is difficult to find a black cat in a dark coal cellar, until it
scratches you. Similarly, it is difficult to negotiate if there are too
many gaps in your knowledge about the situation. You will just find
yourself in a corner.

READING BODY LANGUAGE

We have looked at reading between the lines of what is said, but
words, tone and emphasis are not the only ways messages come over
when we speak with someone. People project all sorts of non-verbal
clues to their feelings. Body language is an inexact science, but interesting and worth some study. One gesture is not an infallible sign of
anything. An unbuttoned jacket may only mean it is a tight fit; wear-
ing a jacket at all may indicate fierce air conditioning rather than for-
mality. However, the checklist that follows provides some guidelines
to what *may* be indicated by what.

Your intention should be not to over-react to anything, or to use
one gesture as an infallible sign, but not to ignore indications that
could be useful either. Proceed with care. See Figure 6 for a checklist of body language.

It is worth keeping an eye on body language through the whole
process of negotiation. Remember, though, that it is only providing
clues and should not become a fixation. There are plenty of other
things to concentrate on.

Example: considering expected behaviour
A meeting is about to take place in Malaysia. A European visitor has
had some correspondence with the general manager of a local organisation and a meeting is arranged. The European is greeted cordially,

Open-mindedness
Shown by:
- open hands
- unbuttoned coat.

Wariness
Shown by:
- arms crossed on chest
- legs over chair arm while seated
- sitting in reversed armless chair
- crossing legs
- fistlike gestures
- pointing index finger
- karate chops.

Thinking/analysing
Shown by:
- hand to face gestures
- head tilted
- stroking chin
- peering over glasses
- taking glasses off, cleaning them
- earpiece of glasses in mouth
- pipe-smoker gestures
- getting up from table, walking around
- putting hand to bridge of nose.

Confidence
Shown by:
- steepling of the hands
- hands on back of head, authority position
- back stiffened
- hands in coat pockets, with thumbs outside
- hands on lapels of coat.

Territorial dominance
Shown by:
- feet on desk
- feet on chair
- leaning against/touching object
- placing object in a desired space
- hands behind head, leaning back.

Nervousness
Shown by:
- clearing throat
- 'whew' sound
- whistling
- cigarette-smoking
- picking/pinching flesh
- fidgeting in chair
- hands covering mouth while speaking
- not looking at the other person
- tugging at trousers or skirt while seated
- jingling money in pockets
- tugging at ear
- perspiration/wringing of hands.

Fig. 6. Body language clues.

Frustration
Shown by:
• short breaths
• tutting sound
• tightly clenched hands
• wringing hands
• fistlike gestures
• pointing index finger
• running hand through hair
• rubbing back of neck.

Boredom
Shown by:
• doodling
• drumming
• legs cross, foot kicking
• head in palms of hands
• blank stare.

Acceptance
Shown by:
• hand to chest
• open arms and hands
• touching gestures
• moving closer to another
• preening.

Expectancy
Shown by:
• rubbing palms
• jingling money
• crossed fingers
• moving closer.

Suspicion
Shown by:
• not looking at you
• arms crossed
• moving away from you
• silhouette body towards you
• sideways glance
• touching/rubbing nose
• rubbing eye(s)
• buttoning coat
• drawing away.

Alertness/attention
Shown by:
• hands on hips
• hands on mid-thigh when seated
• sitting on edge of chair
• arms spread, gripping edge of table/desk
• moving closer
• open hands
• hand to face gestures
• unbuttoning coat
• tilted head.

offered a drink and as the meeting seems about to get under way he is given a business card. He tucks it quickly in his top pocket and begins to state his case.

A small point, but the ritual of business card exchange is an important one in the East. It is expected that you study a card, view it as important and store it safely. Certainly you need to hand over one of your own in exchange. Not doing so will not make the discussion collapse in ruins, but failure to understand local conditions might have a negative effect.

The moral: it pays to check such local differences of behaviour and social nuance. It is one thing to check currency rates and tariffs, it is another to remember not to point your feet at someone in case it causes offence, as in Buddhist countries. This example makes a general point which may stand further investigation if you plan to deal internationally.

Keeping in context
The reason for being sensitive to what is said, nuances, gestures, etc is to help stay in line with the two basic factors of negotiation:

- your plan
- your reading of how things are going and being received.

FINE-TUNING

Negotiation demands constant fine-tuning. Just as in a sailing boat a hand needs to be kept on the tiller to compensate for wind and tide and maintain smooth progress towards a destination, so it is with negotiation. However well planned your tactics, you are constantly having to respond to the other party. Sometimes this means dealing with something you expected, at least at some point and in some form, and which you can be prepared for. On other occasions it means responding quickly to unexpected things.

The overall objective is to remain on course. You are heading towards your objectives whatever happens, though there may need to be some give and take. It is important that any response you make is, whilst prompt, also considered. Some of this can only come with practice. it is always worth analysing what went well, less well and what there is to learn from a negotiation, whatever the outcome.

Reacting to the other party's tactics

The following may help accelerate experience. It indicates some of the tactics you may face and suggests what the other party hopes for as a result, and your possible response.

- *Other party's behaviour*: **chaos** displays anger, storms out, takes umbridge
  Hoping you will: apologise, give concession, or get angry yourself.
  Your action: keep calm, express your concern at any misunderstanding, seek clarification, let things return to normal before trying to proceed.

- *Other party's behaviour*: **poor me** plea for special sympathy, concern or approach because of their situation.
  Hoping you will: give more because you feel sorry for them.
  Your action: do not be put off or be overly sympathetic, acknowledge the problem, restate your position and take the conversation back on track.

- *Other party's behaviour*: **not me** claims they cannot make decision, must refer to boss, spouse, committee.
  Hoping you will: yield to pressure without souring relations: it is not my fault.
  Your action: ask questions to ascertain whether it is true or just a ploy. In some meetings it may be worth checking early on whether they have the authority to make an arrangement.

- *Other party's behaviour*: **only option** keeps suggesting unacceptable option, without alternative.
  Hoping you will: be forced into agreement, seeing no option.
  Your action: keep calm, bear your objectives firmly in mind, suggest other alternatives such as a middle ground, keep setting out the problem.

- *Other party's behaviour*: **no way** immediately stating one element as non-negotiable.
  Hoping you will: give up or offer a great deal to try to make it negotiable.
  Your action: offer to set that element aside, moving on to other things and getting back to it once rapport is established and agreement is clear on some other elements.

- *Other party's behaviour*: **what?** overreaction to something, shock-horror to indicate impasse.

Hoping you will: offer a rapid concession to compensate.
Your action: ignore the first response and restate the issue to prompt a more considered, informative response.

- *Other party's behaviour*: **can't** opens with a problem: we can't do anything unless the project can be completed by the end of the month.   ¹
  Hoping you will: concede
  Your action: question for truth – it is more likely an initial stance – refer to the other variables.

- *Other party's behaviour*: **no-can-do** contains no detail or reason but is very negative: 'That's just not at all acceptable'.
  Hoping you will: see it as intractable and give in.
  Your action: ask for detail, why it is unacceptable, how different it needs to be. Get away from the unspecific and down to the facts.

- *Other party's behaviour*: **something more** an overt request for some extra benefit.
  Hoping you will: give it to gain goodwill and keep things going.
  Your action: investigate the trading possibilities. If I give you X, would you be able to agree to Y?

- *Other party's behaviour*: **policy** the rules are quoted: 'more than my job's worth' eg company policy.
  Hoping you will: read it as unchangeable and not even try to negotiate.
  Your action: check whether it is true, whether there are exceptions or others have authority to make them. Rules are made to be broken but be prepared for this to be difficult on occasion and, if necessary, to leave it.

- *Other party's behaviour*: **sell me** negotiation is dependent on a tacit agreement, eg to buy, action. If the deal is put in question the whole situation may be changing.
  Hoping you will: give in to secure agreement.
  Your action: ask questions, do we go back to the stage of persuasion, or is it a ploy. If so stick to your position and push back hard.

- *Other party's behaviour*: **big vs little** a big deal is made of a small point, then used as a concession for something they really want.
  Hoping you will: see the first as a real issue and trade, in a way

that is not a good exchange.
Your action: check real importance, compare and deal with the two things together.

- *Other party's behaviour*: **no progress** things appear to be dead-locked, no clear way out.
  Hoping you will: give in as only way forward.
  Your action: suggest a real change, a break, an arbitrator. If it is a ploy these may be resisted and you can get back on track.

If you are a regular negotiator it may be worth keeping notes of your own examples, as an *aide memoire* for the future.

Getting results
There are several aspects to negotiation. The process itself is important, the structure and sequence of events contribute to its success. The ritual may be important, the techniques certainly are, but it is ultimately *people* that make it work, so no aspect of interpersonal behaviour must be overlooked.

Any difficulty is likely to be less because the individual elements are themselves complex, than because of the problem of orchestrating the whole thing. Those who get every aspect moving together effectively are likely to make the best negotiators.

CHECKLIST

1. Concentrate throughout any negotiation meeting. There will always be a great deal to take in.

2. Keep your ears and eyes open for any sign, any nuance, that might assist you in the process.

3. Remember that behavioural factors can give warning of dangers, allowing you to take action to avoid them, and highlight opportunities, allowing you to strengthen the effectiveness of what you do.

CASE STUDY

John makes use of interpersonal behaviour
John is a department head in a busy local government office. Certain matters have to be agreed by his superior, James, before he can pro-

ceed on them alone. The two generally work well together, partly through experience and getting the measure of each other. John understands, for example, the amount of detail his boss needs to see before letting go.

One fault James has is that he hates to say no, even when it is right to do so. He will talk and talk until time and the fact that they are both busy leads to it being left. Today he is doing just that, endlessly bypassing a decision about something John wants to get under way fast.

John decides to meet the issue head on. Once it is clear what is happening, he stands up.

'Perhaps I should forget it,' he looks his colleague straight in the eye, 'but you do want to get the appraisal system revised before the year end, don't you?'

James is brought up short, both by the action and the fact that the question relates to something quite different from their discussion.

'Yes, of course,' he said, 'That's surely agreed.'

John interrupts, 'Yes, it is, but we are never going to achieve it if this other matter isn't cleared up fast. Now what I suggest is . . .'

John has taken command, reset the agenda and now has much more likelihood of getting a decision. This was not because of what was said, though this may have helped. It was through the impact of something purely behavioural. Just saying it politely would not have had the same impact. This is just one aspect of the power of inter-personal behaviour in negotiating.

DISCUSSION POINTS

1. How can you use behavioural factors to avoid dangers that are created for you in negotiation?

2. Similarly, how can you spot opportunities to increase your power and influence in negotiation using such factors?

3. What particular factors do you think you can identify and use that play to your style and strengths?

6
Reaching Agreement

'The big print giveth and the fine print taketh away.'

J. Fulton Sheen

FINDING THE RIGHT FORMAT

Some negotiations, however hard fought, are essentially informal. No elaborate record is necessary, both parties are content to implement whatever has been agreed. It may be an essentially transient arrangement and once over is quickly forgotten.

Other negotiations need to state clear arrangements, without having to be in writing. It should, though, be noted that a **verbal contract** can be binding in a court of law. Consider this category very carefully. Make sure nothing more formal is necessary. Formalities are less necessary when all goes well, then goodwill will see things through. They are to catch situations that change or cannot be foreseen such as, for example, a change of personnel in a company.

With other negotiations the arrangements need documenting. The setting out of **terms and conditions**, or other arrangements, is intended to be formal, contractual and is very necessary. Once agreed the parties are stuck with them. No review of negotiating would therefore be complete without some comment on this aspect of the process. When it is necessary it can be very important to get it right. Omissions here can cost dear.

DECIDING THE PURPOSE OF A CONTRACT

The intention of a **contract** is protective. It secures against what might happen if agreement is not implemented. Sometimes the penalty is considerable; if terms and conditions are not met a significant amount of money may be lost.

For example, if you book a wedding reception, then the bride and groom fall out and there is no wedding, there may still be a large bill to pay. The venue owners, unable to relet the facility at short notice, are protecting themselves against loss of income.

Making contracts acceptable.

For a contractual situation to be acceptable, and not seen as inappropriate, draconian or otherwise unsuitable, certain factors are important. If you are introducing it, make sure that what you do:

- is communicated clearly with no possibility of misunderstandings
- enhances the relationship involved, if necessary on a continuing basis
- allows the progressing and securing of agreement to proceed effectively and promptly
- still allows any necessary flexibility within the arrangement
- links logically and neatly to the practicalities involved.

SETTING POLICY

In an organisation of any size the first question may be who makes policy decisions and with whom they consult. If you are in charge of such matters, fine; if not you may still have an input to make. Look out for any circumstances not covered by existing policy and be ready to feed back information that may prompt policy change or update.

An example, is the wedding reception referred to above. It may be decided that stricter terms and conditions, and penalties for cancellation, are necessary at certain times of year. A wedding function lost in, say, July is perhaps more damaging than at other times as this is peak season.

Addressing the essentials

Contractual arrangements need to make clear:

- the basis of the agreement
- the terminology to be used by both parties (eg is postponement different from cancellation?)
- all elements of timing
- the procedures, documentation and administration involved
- all financial matters in detail.

INTRODUCING CONTRACTUAL MATTERS

A contract may cause problems if it also causes surprise. Produce a ten-page document for signature after hours of debate and discussion that contained no mention of the need for it, and people will twitch. Make matters clear from the beginning.

- Do not apologise for the arrangement, though you may need to explain its necessity.

- Stress the *mutual* advantages.

- Use language that stresses the joint benefits of clarity, eg talk about working together.

- Plan to mention the contractual side progressively, sufficiently early, and set the scene for any detailed discussion about it that may be necessary later.

- Use a checklist to ensure no detail is missed. Make sure all necessary information is to hand, or secured and recorded if it is to be part of the agreement.

The process is progressive and dealing with it may well be spread throughout the meeting.

DEALING WITH CONTRACTUAL MATTERS

This is often a crucial element of many negotiation discussions. A systematic approach to handling it may therefore be useful.

Working step-by-step

The following ten key points will help you plan and implement this aspect into the whole of the proceedings.

1. Introduce the concept of contract

This needs to be carefully timed. The right moment may pass, and it then gets more difficult to say: 'We must have this in writing.' Waiting for the other party to raise things may not be best; you have to plan and be prepared to move the conversation onto the matter. A first mention may simply aim to gain agreement on the need for discussion on it. It may also decide how and when in the discussion this will be done.

2. Make sure details are clear

This is an area for crystal clear communication. Different interpretations of one word – when does provisional become permanent? – may cause disproportionately great problems later.

3. Make figures and timing especially clear
Both these are worth being really pedantic about. When, exactly, is the end of the month or year? Again, misunderstanding of such a detail can cause real problems.

4. Check understanding
This may be as simple as just saying 'Is that clear' occasionally, but it is very important. Don't just *think* matters are clearly understood between you. You need to *know*.

5. Document your side of arrangements
Make things clear, agree them, then say how you will confirm it and do just that. Delays can cause confusion. It may also help precision of agreement if you take the initiative: write in detail, then they can simply say they agree. Sometimes you may want to do this the other way round to save you time, with a supplier for example, but read the small print carefully.

6. Ask for their confirmation
Do not assume this will come: ask. Chase it if necessary. If contractual arrangements are understood and agreed, you do not have to be circumspect about this.

7. Chase for action
This is crucial. If people ignore some key stage, do not feel awkward about reminding them. Make sure you do not forget, put a note in the diary if matters stretch over some time. Delay might well be in the other party's interest.

9. Adopt the right manner
Always take a positive approach to contractual matters, stressing that they are important and help both parties. Deal with them in a way that appears efficient, professional and will achieve what you want in the smoothest possible way.

10. Link to the future
An agreement and contract made today set the scene for the future. You may want to begin to touch on future arrangements as you tie down a current one. This can pay dividends in the long run.

Being on the receiving end
You will not always be the one introducing contractual matters, of course. When such things are put to you the rules are straightforward:

- Listen, read and check everything that is put over, to make sure you truly understand.

- Take time, if necessary, to consider or to confer with someone else including, if appropriate, a legal mind.

- Be absolutely sure that you can live with the implications, including those of the worst case scenario, *before* you sign anything.

TACKLING BREAKDOWN

If you deal with contractual matters in the right kind of way there should be minimal problems. But what if something contractual is agreed and then the other party fails to comply in some way? There are three options.

Applying the letter of the law
The first option is simply to stick to the terms exactly. That is what they are there for. They were agreed. There is no need to feel bad about invoking the conditions. Sometimes this approach will go unchallenged and cause no problems. If not, or if you are yourself worried about souring future arrangements, you may need to take other action.

Negotiating a compromise
Secondly, if you feel so inclined you can insist on less than the full terms. You may make some other arrangement that will foster good-will without your losing anything significant. If the situation is reversed you may want to insist this is done, to minimise damage to yourself.

Making an exception
This third option is really a variant of the compromise above. It may be important to make it clear that what is done is an exception setting no precedents for the future. If this point is strongly made it may be felt that you are being very reasonable, and this may lead to return compromise in future.

The trick here is to balance avoiding immediate losses with advantages of a more long-term nature.

CHECKLIST

1. Decide appropriate policy and introduce contractual matters into any meeting in a way that sets the scene for what you want to do.

2. Be sensitive to the details involved and ensure mutual understanding of the full picture.

3. Adopt a systematic approach to the way contractual matters are integrated into the discussion.

4. Check and check again before you sign anything.

5. Balance advantages/disadvantages in terms of the severity with which you apply the letter of the law, if this proves necessary.

CASE STUDY

Charles and Jackie think they have agreed

Charles works for a government agency giving advice and providing support services in developing countries. He has people going to and fro undertaking projects in a dozen countries. He is meeting with a sales executive of an international hotel group to secure a corporate rate that will save money, yet allow him to accommodate his people suitably.

Jackie is the sales executive. She is keen to do a deal, and knows there is a worthwhile amount of business to be had if she does.

Their meeting looks at the volume of business, the locations involved, the rates and discounts involved, the facilities included. For example, Charles needs to be sure his people can operate computers and faxes in their rooms.

Using the ploy of concentrating on the rates, and the savings he must make, Charles gets Jackie to the point of doing a deal, then throws in a last-minute request: 'Of course, this would only be acceptable if the arrangement guaranteed executive grade rooms'. Jackie vaguely agrees. She sees the profitability of the deal declining and kicks herself for letting the ploy work. Her last word on the matter is non-committal: 'I'll see what I can do.' When they part, each is content that the deal agreed works for them.

Much later Charles notices in a fax from one of his people in Africa that, just as the new arrangement should be under way, they found only a basic grade of room was reserved for them. As a result the fax had had to be sent through the hotel switchboard and was delayed some hours.

Getting things in writing

Why the problem? Simple; there was nothing in writing. Or, at least nothing that set out the full details point by point. Charles thought he had prompted an extra concession by using a clever ploy. Jackie, who had not actually promised anything, thought it had been forgotten and done no more about it.

Even in so simple a situation, such a failing (and both parties here were at fault) can cause problems. In this case it may only necessitate a small change to the arrangement. But even if Jackie now includes the upgrade, will Charles ever be quite so happy about the deal? It will no doubt change the situation when the contract needs renewing a year hence.

It is easy to imagine the possible confusion when much more detailed contractual arrangements are part of negotiation.

DISCUSSION POINTS

1. What points need deciding and including in any policy for contractual matters you may have?

2. Do you have clear information available as a prompt to discussion – a checklist, for example – to ensure you do not miss any tricks?

3. How much documentation does your situation demand and does it need origination or review?

7
Learning from Experience

'What we have to learn to do, we learn by doing.'

Aristotle

FOCUSING ON THE KEY ISSUES

Negotiation is part art, part science. Going about it in the right way increases the likelihood of success. However, it does not guarantee it. It is a dynamic, interactive process. It needs to be conducted in a way that is well planned, yet flexible, that recognises that the people element is the most important – and the least predictable.

The danger with dissecting any such process is that it can then be difficult to put the pieces together. Now it is time to pull together the essentials.

ORCHESTRATING THE OVERALL PROCESS

To negotiate successfully you must see the process in the round, take a broad view and continue to do so throughout the process. This means you must have a good grasp of the principles involved, for it is that which allows you the opportunity to orchestrate and fine-tune the process as you proceed. Small adjustments as you progress can make all the difference.

Summarising the principles

1. Definition: negotiation is about bargaining to reach a mutually agreeable outcome. This is the win-win concept.

2. Never neglect your preparation. Have a clear plan but remain flexible.

3. Participants must regard each other as equals. Mutual respect is essential to both conduct and outcome.

4. There is a need to abide by the rules. Negotiation is about discussion, rather than debate. There is little place for overt one-upmanship or domination, yet each must fight their corner.

5. Put your cards on the table, at least on major issues. Do not pretend powers or state intentions that are untrue.

6. Patience is a key characteristic of the good negotiator. Take your time, do not rush discussion or decision making. Delay is better than a poor outcome.

7. Empathy is vital. Put yourself in the other's shoes, see things objectively from their point of view.

8. State clear objectives. Being open early on about overall intentions can save groping in the dark.

9. Avoid confrontation. Do not get into a corner you cannot get out of. Avoid rows and showdowns, but stand firm and keep calm.

10. Treat disagreement carefully. Act as devil's advocate, apparently looking at the case from the other's viewpoint, to avoid a confrontational 'I disagree' style.

11. Deal with concessions progressively. Where concessions have to be made, make them unwillingly and one at a time – and trade them.

12. Do not let perfection be the enemy of the good. An outcome that is one hundred per cent what you want is rarely an option. Be realistic, do not waste time and effort seeking something out of reach.

13. Use openness but not comprehensively. Declaring your plans and intentions may be useful to the discussion. You may want to keep hidden the motivation behind them.

14. Stick with your objectives. Set your sights high and settle as high as possible. Know when to drop the whole thing rather than agree a totally inappropriate deal.

15. Keep up your guard. Maintain your stamina, bide your time. The other party may persevere for hours to see when you will crack.

16. Remain professional. For example, respect confidences that are given in the course of negotiations. Such consideration builds relationships and may help you next time.

17. Never underestimate people. A velvet glove may be disguising an iron fist.

18. End positively. Neither party will get exactly what they want, but if the deal is agreeable emphasise this at the end.

Summarising the tactics

Like any interactive skill negotiating is dependent on a plethora of factors. The following are picked to provide a top ten of things likely to be most useful. You might like to compose your own list, see how it varies and make sure it reflects exactly the kind of negotiating you do and the kind of people it pits you against.

1. Select the right starting point. Your plan should make it easy for you to take the initiative and quickly get onto your agenda.

2. Aim high, then the trading moves you less far from what you regard as a good position.

3. Do not make your feelings obvious. There is an element of bluff. If your face and body language say 'this is minor' as you respond to something major you will do better.

4. Use silence. Some things demand no reaction at all.

5. Watch for early difficulty. Let a rapport and momentum build up before you tackle contentious issues.

6. Do not exaggerate facts. They can be verified and exaggeration causes problems later.

7. Communicate clearly. Remember the need for understanding as a foundation to the whole process.

8. Be seen to go with the other person's way of doing things, at least to some degree and particularly if you are on their ground.

9. Do not push too hard. There is usually a line beyond which the outcome is not a better deal, but complete breakdown.

10. When negotiation is finished, stop. Once agreement is reached, clear, agreed and perhaps noted, move on to other matters. Otherwise people say 'I have been thinking . . .' and you are back to square one.

The importance of different factors like these depends on the nature of the negotiation. Something full of complex financial details poses different problems from something simpler.

ENHANCING YOUR APPROACH

A few things to avoid. You will only excel if you never:

- over-react if responses are negative; the other person is at pains *not* to say how excellent every point is
- allow yourself to become over-emotional, unpleasant, provocative or insulting; a planned and controlled display of emotion may be useful, but you must know what you are doing
- agree to something you do not want; in many situations there is a minimal deal which your plan should identify, below which it is better to walk away.

Learning from each situation

Every negotiating situation can teach you something: what works well, what to avoid, what best fits your style. The detail is important. Sometimes what makes the difference between success and failure is small and seemingly insignificant. One phrase, even one gesture may make such a difference. If all the details are right, the whole will be more likely to work well.

PRODUCING REAL CLOUT

Negotiation is a topic about which no guide can be comprehensive. It is a dynamic, interactive, process and even the best performance can be made more effective. The key things are to start, and ensure that the experience you gain makes what you do in future better and better.

Remember when you learnt to drive, or to juggle with flaming torches? You probably despaired of ever being able to concentrate on a disparate, long, list of things all at once, and make it work.

Negotiation is no different. A basic shopping list of techniques will start you off and allow you to practise. Then with the basic techniques in mind you can add to your method of approach and continue to develop it.

Such conscious use of experience in the light of your awareness and knowledge of the process is the only way to develop real clout. You cannot expect that to come overnight, or without thought or practise.

MAKING RESOLUTIONS FOR THE FUTURE

Finally, a few things are worth emphasising about this process of developing skills.

Preparation is key

Preparation really does make a significant difference. Yet it is so easy to miss out, or skimp. Make time for it, think about it, and everything else that follows will be easier.

Being aware of the process

Secondly, try to develop a consciousness of the process. If your mind is actively aware of the overall issues, the complexities and the structure of what is involved, rather than simply moving from point to point, the whole process will be easier. This may seem difficult to begin with. A chess player will concentrate on the current move in the context of the next, the one after, and the opponent's response, all within an overall strategy; it is important in negotiation too. It does work and becomes easier with practice. In time both the learning process and the deployment of the many techniques will become a habit.

Becoming confident

Thirdly, remember that confidence is paramount. Planning is the starting point for this. If you have thought about both the principles and the detail of a particular encounter, you will have more confidence in what you plan to do. This will not only help you, it will be apparent to your opponent and you will come across in a way that will make the whole process easier.

We are, I hope, agreed that you can be a better negotiator if you work at it. Indeed, the process of trying will itself help you learn quicker and do better. Continue this process for a while and you will be a match for anyone.

CHECKLIST

1. Work from a real understanding of the key principles involved in the negotiation process.

2. Always see the process as dynamic. Work throughout any meeting to fine-tune how you proceed.

3. Stand back and retain the broad view of what is going on, so that you can spot and avoid any pitfalls.

4. Consciously use your experience to enhance your approach and maximise what you achieve.

CASE STUDY

Michael seeks promotion

Michael is preparing to go into a meeting with his boss, with the possibility of being promoted. He works in middle management for a financial institution, successfully running a small department. He believes he deserves promotion both on the basis of his success to date, and his ability to tackle a more demanding job.

Michael knows that the industry he is in has been through dramatic change, including reduced staff levels, in recent years. He knows the demands that higher responsibility will make on him, and wants to be sure that he is suitably rewarded for it. He also knows that the organisation is currently successful and profitable. In a technical business it makes sense to 'grow your own management, but he wonders just what this means. Will they be prepared to negotiate, or quickly decide it is better to recruit from outside or select someone else to promote if he pushes for too much?

Gill wants the right person

Gill is the personnel director. She wants to make the right decisions, to ensure that the post is filled in a way that will meet the objectives of the job and without disturbing personnel policy or costing too much.

Both parties plan their approach

Michael knows enough to plan for the meeting. He considers himself and his strengths relative to the new job, the task itself and the package he considers appropriate. Such a package has plenty of variables:

salary, car, expenses, bonuses, medical insurance, pension arrangements, etc. He also considers things like his new location, staff support, freedom of action, reporting hierarchy and other matters which affect him and his perception of his ability to do a good job.

Next Michael considers his approach and what it will say about him. Too strong and he will be thought to be difficult; too soft and the personnel director will wonder why these things do not matter to him. He prioritises the variables: what is a must, etc. He makes some notes, sets an agenda and goes into the meeting ready and confident. He believes he has thought through all the likely scenarios, not least from the point of view of what the other person will do.

Gill also prepares. She wants to be able to confirm the appointment. She too thinks through all that is involved, where to put the emphasis, and is ready and confident.

Both parties want something good for the company, yet are in a sense adversaries, at least for a while. They are probably equally matched, which reinforces the need for attention to detail in order to secure an edge. A win-win outcome is desirable for both. Michael wants to be able to accept the job and get on with it without regrets about the package. Gill wants him to accept, move into the new appointment able to give it his full attention. Their aims are not so different.

The way they conduct themselves will affect the outcome Whatever the conclusion, it will not be something that just happened. It will depend on the skills of both and how they each deploy the techniques involved in communication generally, and negotiation in particular. *They* will make the outcome what it is.

MOVING INTO THE REAL WORLD

As with the case above, so too for you. How well your next negotiating session turns out will depend as much as anything on you. This book has set out to act as a spur to your abilities, but it is what you do now that matters. What you are *able* to do depends very much on how consciously you set about it. You need to understand and deploy the techniques appropriately. You also need confidence in your ability to do so effectively.

Good luck is what makes *other* people's negotiations succeed. *You* are what makes yours succeed. I wish you well with them.

DISCUSSION POINTS

1. How do you prepare and plan the best approach?

2. How do you deploy the techniques that can best help you achieve your aims?

3. How do you make sure you remain quick on your feet throughout the process?

4. How do you stand back to see the broad picture, yet miss no detail as you orchestrate the whole process?

Appendix: An Exercise in Negotiation

Reading a book is, normally speaking, a solitary activity. Yet negotiation is, of course, by its nature interactive. If reading the book has whetted your appetite to try out some of the techniques reviewed, and if you are tired of 'Trivial Pursuit', the following exercise will give you some idea of your current facility for negotiating effectively.

You will need a friend or colleague to do the exercise with you (or, to produce a more complex situation, two teams of, say, three or four, in which case planning may take a little longer as you must agree and allocate roles – imagine, if you like, that a team of three is the couple owning the house and their architect – and decide who will do what. When people are ready, proceed as follows:

1. All or both of you read the following:

   Imagine A and B are having a house built virtually on the same site. They are, let us imagine, doing the work themselves, and in some ways, have made a poor start. A while into the work each finds that what they have assembled – materials, equipment and labour – is ill matched to the task.

   To reduce the time and cost of development they have decided to *negotiate* with each other about sharing resources, some of which each has in surplus, some of which they are short of to complete the work.

   The exercise is actually to carry out the negotiation and see how satisfactory an outcome can be achieved.

2. Each person (or team) should now read *one* of the briefs that follow and *not* look at the other. Brief A appears on page 95, and B on page 96, each set of information is different and you need to decide how and when to disclose and use the information in the coming discussion.

3. Once the separate briefs have been read, allow about 10 minutes to think through *individually* what you will do (make a few notes, perhaps).

4. With planning complete, allow 20–30 minutes for discussion.

5. After discussion, when an arrangement has – hopefully – been made, refer to the summary of the exercise on page 97, and total the financial value of your achieved position.

BRIEF A

Your situation is shown below. Note that each element of resources has been given a 'unit value' to keep things simple. The values will act as a measure of what is to be negotiated. Some are close to what you need; others are far apart and there is a gap to be closed. Additionally some items are designated as 'priorities', and you receive a higher score in the end if you achieve a good balance with them. (Each team has different priorities, and you should not therefore assume that the other team's intentions are as yours). The variables thus represent any mixed group of different, and differently valued, elements which might be involved in any negotiation. So 20 'units' of bricks might be tons, 3 'units' of cement mixing might be hours or days of work capacity – only the relative values matter. You should take as priorities labour and glass (marked with an asterisk below).

Resources	Units available	Units needed
Timber	6	12
Bricks	20	7
Copper pipe	10	12
Labour*	9	15
Cement mixing	3	9
Glass*	5	11
Plaster	16	3
Plumbing fittings	8	16

As a guide to the relative value of the arrangement you make, bear in mind the following:
- you save £1000 for every needed unit passed to you by B
- you save £1000 for every surplus unit you pass to B
- for resources marked with an asterisk, the saving is £3000
- for each resource area where you achieve balance, i.e. units available are exactly what you need, add a £2000 bonus.

BRIEF B

Your situation is shown below. Note that each element of resources has been given a 'unit value' to keep things simple. The values will act as a measure of what is to be negotiated. Some are close to what you need; others are far apart and there is a gap to be closed. Additionally some items are designated as 'priorities', and you receive a higher score in the end if you achieve a good balance with them. (Each team has different priorities, and you should not therefore assume that the other team's intentions are as yours.) The variables thus represent any mixed group of different, and differently valued, elements which might be involved in any negotiation. So 6 'units' of bricks might be tons, 5 'units' of cement mixing might be hours or days of work capacity – only the relative values matter. You should take as priorities cement mixing and plumbing fittings (marked with an asterisk below).

Resources	Units available	Units needed
Timber	20	7
Bricks	6	14
Copper pipe	10	12
Labour	15	9
Cement mixing*	5	11
Glass	3	9
Plaster	4	10
Plumbing fittings*	16	3

As a guide to the relative value of the arrangement you make bear in mind the following:
• you save £1000 for every needed unit passed to you by A
• you save £1000 for every surplus unit you pass to A
• for resources marked with an asterisk, the saving is £3000
• for each resource area where you achieve balance, i.e. units available are exactly what you need, add a £2000 bonus.

EXERCISE SUMMARY

Each side should end up with as many elements as possible balanced between what is available and what is needed, and as high a financial total as possible. The following chart, shows the variables that are there to be 'tracked'.

	A			B		
	Available	*Needed*	*Surplus*	*Available*	*Needed*	*Surplus*
Timber	6	12	–6	20	7	+13
Bricks	20	7	+13	6	14	–8
Copper pipe	10	12	–2	10	12	–2
Labour	9	15	–6	15	9	+6
Cement mixing	3	9	–6	5	11	–6
Glass	5	11	–6	3	9	–6
Plaster	16	3	+13	4	10	–6
Plumbing fittings	8	16	–8	16	3	+13

How did you do? With the benefit of hindsight, did you do enough planning (particularly if working in teams)? Did you achieve a good mix, or just isolated victories? Did you exchange willingly? Did you handle it openly or secretly? Did your, manner help or hinder? And can you identify things you should have done differently and would you do better another time? If nothing else, the exercise may persuade you to practise!

Glossary

Body language. Signs evident through position or gesture that suggest, but do not guarantee, the state of mind of the other person.

Bridges. Something that provides an element of agreement or a common basis for discussion.

Concessions. Used interchangeably with variable. Indicates those aspects of any deal that must be arranged and agreed during the course of negotiation.

Empathy. The ability to put yourself in another person's place and see things from their point of view, and importantly in context of negotiating to *be seen to do so.*

Flagging. Indicating what is to come, or the nature of what is to come (also referred to as singposting).

History of contact. The past communication and how it affects the current relationship and discussions.

Icebergs. Hidden motives that condition what is being said and how it is put.

Initial stance. The starting point adopted by a party in negotiating, not necessarily close to where they will end up.

Neutrality. Used in the sense of not appearing to favour a particular outcome or position.

Objectives. Desired results. They should be specific and measurable, and linked to time, rather than vague or grandiose intentions.

Ploy. Something used to distract and create an edge.

Point of balance. The place, somewhere between the extremes of possibilities, where agreement can be made.

Power. Factors, tangible or otherwise, that give one person some sort of edge.

Promise of reward. Factor offered to improve the deal for the other party.

Signposting. See flagging.

Stance. The position taken up by a negotiator at any particular stage or over any particular issue. Stances can change progressively.

Strategy. A course of action designed to achieve specific objectives.
Tactics. The precise methods used to implement a strategy.
Threat of punishment. Factors that can potentially reduce the balance of advantage.
Trading. The process of arranging, and sometimes exchanging, concessions. This is an inherent element of the negotiation process.
Variable. The raw material of trading; see concessions.
Win-win. A common way of referring to a satisfactory outcome for both parties.

Further Reading

There are many books on the subject of negotiation, many covering the same ground in different ways. It is always worth revisiting a topic and doing so can strengthen understanding, which in turn can make putting techniques to work easier and more certain.

Two good texts are:

Getting to Yes, Roger Fisher and William Ury (Arrow Business Books, 1987)

Putting it across, Angela Heylin (Michael Joseph).

The other books listed here are complementary and will help add to the knowledge that makes successful negotiation possible.

The Negotiator's Tactic Bank – this carries no authors name, though, for the record, the author of this book was one of the contributors – (Wyvern Crest Publications 1997). This is a ring binder of techniques, 201 of them. Each is set out in similar style presenting the circumstances and purpose to which they are directed, and – in mini-case form – something about exactly how to use them. It makes an excellent companion to a book like this which reviews the overall process. A paperback version is available of just 70 of the techniques from the main volume under the title *Negotiating Tactics*.

Balance Sheet Barrier, The, Anthony Jay (Video Arts, 1977). The booklet that supports one of the Video Arts' John Cleese training films.

Body Language, Allan Pease (Sheldon Press, 1988 and subsequently revised).

How to Communicate at Work, Ann Dobson (How To Books, 1995).

How to Read a Balance Sheet (International Labour Office, Geneva). A classic, arranged in programmed learning style it can hardly fail to leave anyone better informed.

Mastering Business English, Michael Bennie (How To Books, 1996).

Negotiation: Tying the Knot (Video Arts, 1996). An excellent short film taking a general view of negotiation. Its supporting booklet, same title, is useful too as a quick reference.

101 Ways to Increase Sales, Patrick Forsyth (Kogan Page, 1996). A quick, practical view of the essential techniques.

Ready Made Activities for Negotiation Skills, Sheila Cane (Pitman Publishing, 1994) A practical guide that will enable you to put together a general course on the subject.

Useful Addresses

Negotiation is a skill with broad business and general application, so contact points that might link with it would make a long list. The following highlights a number of specialist organisations.

TRAINING

More than 700 organisations offer public courses in the UK alone and more offer in-house training. The following can offer advice on which course is right for which requirement:

National Training Index, 4 New Burlington Street, London W1X 2HX. Tel: (0171) 494 1268.

MANAGEMENT

Professional management bodies offer advice, training, have libraries, journals, etc. The two most relevant are:

The Institute of Management, Cottingham Road, Corby, Northamptonshire NN17 1TT. Tel: (01536) 204222.
The Chartered Institute of Marketing, Moor Hall, Cookham Maidenhead, Berkshire SL6 9QH. Tel: (01628) 427333.

PROFESSIONAL HELP

Some kinds of negotiation may require a professional input from outsiders.
The Chartered Institute of Arbitrators, 24 Angel Gate, City Road, London EC1V. Tel: (0171) 837 4483.
Advisory, Conciliation and Arbitration Service, 83 Euston Road, London EC1. Tel: (0171) 396 5100.

BUSINESS LIBRARY

Most libraries include business material and there are ones linked to management organisations. The most specific one is:

City Business Library, 1 Brewers Hall Gardens, London EC2. Tel: (0171) 638 8215.

Index

Afterword

Just one more thing. If you are the kind of person who starts flicking through a book from the back, and are still in the shop deciding whether to purchase a copy or not, then I would repeat the last paragraph of the Preface ... "Of course, I want you to buy this book. You want to be a more effective negotiator. The book will help you do just that. Buy it and we both get what we want. Is it a deal?"

CONDUCTING STAFF APPRAISALS
A practical handbook for every manager today
Nigel Hunt

Managers and organisations neglect staff appraisal at their peril today. But what exactly is staff appraisal? Is it something to be welcomed or feared? Why is it now so vital, and what are the benefits? Should senior as well as junior staff undergo appraisal, and how could this be done? Which managers should do the appraisals, and how should they start? This book, now in a new edition, sets out a basic framework which every manager can use or adapt, whether in business and industry, transport, education, health and public services. Nigel Hunt is a consultant in occupational testing, selection, appraisal, vocational assessment, and management development. He is a Graduate Member of the British Psychological Society, and Associate Member of the Institute of Personnel & Development. 'Informative... Points for discussion and case studies are prominent throughout... the case studies are highly relevant and good.' *Progress* (*NEBS Management Association Journal*). 'Not all books live up to their promises. This one does. At the price it is a bargain.' *British Journal of Administrative Management.*

154pp. illus. 1 85703 399 X.   3rd edition

HOW TO COUNSEL PEOPLE AT WORK
A practical approach to staff care
John Humphries

The value of counselling has become much better recognised in recent times, as a tool for addressing a whole variety of human situations. This book has been specially written for everyone wanting to know how to make use of counselling techniques in the workplace. It discusses what is counselling, the role of the counsellor, communication skills, body language/verbal behaviour, styles of counselling, managing counselling interviews, and the uses of counselling. The book is complete with helpful checklists, case studies, self-assessment material and points for discussion, key addresses, glossary and index.

104pp. illus. 1 85703 093 1.

HOW TO MANAGE PEOPLE AT WORK
A practical guide to effective leadership

John Humphries

'These days, if a textbook on people management is to succeed, it must be highly informative, reliable, comprehensive — and eminently user friendly. Without doubt, *How to Manage People at Work* is one such book. Written in an attractive style that should appeal to any first line manager who has neither the time nor the energy to cope with heavy reading, John Humphries has tackled his extremely wide subject ably and well. Rightly or wrongly, it has always been my experience that one has only to read the first couple of pages of any textbook on people management to discover whether or not the author enjoys an empathy with the people at the sharp end — and here is one author who, for my money, has passed the test with flying colours.' *Progress/NEBS Management Association.*

160pp. illus. 1 85703 068 0.   2nd edition.

ORGANISING EFFECTIVE TRAINING
How to plan and run successful courses and seminars

James Chalmers

Industry, public services, colleges, community groups, and organisations of all kinds urgently need to train their people in a wide variety of much needed skills. But however knowledgeable the tutors are, if a training event has been badly organised it will be a waste of everyone's time and money. This book explains how to plan and organise really successful training events. The method can be applied to anything, from team building to technical courses, and from a one hour briefing up to events lasting several days. The step-by-step approach is easy to follow, and will work equally well with organisers who are unfamiliar with the subject to be trained, as well as professional trainers. If you are ever asked to put on an event, or if you want someone to run one for you, then this will give all the necessary guidance and ensure a successful outcome every time. James Chalmers BSc CEng MIEE has worked in industry for 25 years, and has much experience of running successful training programmes.

160pp. illus. 1 85703 329 9.

MANAGING PROJECTS
How to plan, implement and achieve specific objectives

James Chalmers

The ability to manage projects has become an essential addition to the more traditional management skills. As hierarchies become flatter there is an increasing need for cross-functional cooperation in teams. This book demystifies project management by explaining in a clear and logical manner the techniques needed to manage projects of all sizes. So whether you are planning to move your office, launch a new product, develop a new service, even organise a wedding, this book will show you how to achieve your objective within agreed time, cost and quality targets. James Chalmers Bsc C Eng MIEE has had 25 years experience in service and engineering industries, and has been involved with a large number of successful projects, both large and small. He is author of *Organising Effective Training* in this series.

144pp. illus. 1 85703 378 7.

HOW TO COMMUNICATE AT WORK
Making a success of your working relationships

Ann Dobson

Things only get done properly at work if everyone communicates effectively – whatever their individual role in the organisation. This very practical step-by-step guide gets to the very basics of good communication – what it is and why we need it, how to speak and listen, how to ask and answer questions, how to take messages and use the telephone; how to liaise, negotiate, persuade, offer advice and accept criticism; how to stand up for yourself, dealing with shyness, a difficult boss or angry customer; how to use and understand body language properly, how to cope with visitors, how to store and present information, how to use the English language correctly – and a great deal more, illustrated throughout with examples and case studies. Written by an experienced office staff trainer this book will be a real help to all young people starting a new job, or older individuals returning to work after time away.

192pp illus. 1 85703 103 2.

CONDUCTING EFFECTIVE INTERVIEWS
How to prepare and how to achieve the right outcomes

Ann Dobson

At one time only senior management would carry out interviews. Nowadays, however, effective delegation in large organisations, coupled with the number of small businesses being set up, means that more and more working people at all levels are becoming involved in interviewing. Whether you are interviewing a job applicant, dealing with disciplinary procedures or organising a decision-making session, this book will provide you with all the information you need to achieve your aims. Part 1 offers a step-by-step guide to the general principles of interviewing and Part 2 illustrates the various types of interviews you may be involved with in your working life. Case studies are used to show how the same interview can be dealt with in a successful or unsuccessful way. Ann Dobson is Principal of a Secretarial Training School, and has had long professional experience of interview techniques in theory and practice.

128pp. illus. 1 85703 223 3.

MANAGING MEETINGS
How to prepare, how to take part and how to follow up

Ann Dobson

Meetings can be interesting, productive and even fun! That is the message this 'How To' book seeks to convey. Meetings form a large part of our lives today, particularly in the business world, yet many of us feel ill equipped to handle them with ease. The book is divided into two parts: the first covers the key skills of communicating effectively, motivating and persuading, problem solving, decision making, body language, and dealing with troublemakers. Part 2 deals with the practical steps of holding a meeting and following up. Case studies, self assessment material and checklists complete the simple, yet effective approach. Ann Dobson is Principal of a Secretarial Training School, and has been involved with meetings of varying types for many years. She is also the author of *How to Communicate at Work, Writing Business Letters, How to Return to Work* and *How to Manage an Office* in this series.

124pp. illus. 1 85703 222 5.

How To Books

How To Books provide practical help on a large range of topics. They are available through all good bookshops or can be ordered direct from the distributors. Just tick the titles you want and complete the form on the following page.

___ Apply to an Industrial Tribunal (£7.99)
___ Applying for a Job (£8.99)
___ Applying for a United States Visa (£15.99)
___ Backpacking Round Europe (£8.99)
___ Be a Freelance Journalist (£8.99)
___ Be a Freelance Secretary (£8.99)
___ Become a Freelance Sales Agent (£9.99)
___ Become an Au Pair (£8.99)
___ Becoming a Father (£8.99)
___ Buy & Run a Shop (£8.99)
___ Buy & Run a Small Hotel (£8.99)
___ Buying a Personal Computer (£9.99)
___ Career Networking (£8.99)
___ Career Planning for Women (£8.99)
___ Cash from your Computer (£9.99)
___ Choosing a Nursing Home (£9.99)
___ Choosing a Package Holiday (£8.99)
___ Claim State Benefits (£9.99)
___ Collecting a Debt (£9.99)
___ Communicate at Work (£7.99)
___ Conduct Staff Appraisals (£7.99)
___ Conducting Effective Interviews (£8.99)
___ Coping with Self Assessment (£9.99)
___ Copyright & Law for Writers (£8.99)
___ Counsel People at Work (£7.99)
___ Creating a Twist in the Tale (£8.99)
___ Creative Writing (£9.99)
___ Critical Thinking for Students (£8.99)
___ Dealing with a Death in the Family (£9.99)
___ Do Your Own Advertising (£8.99)
___ Do Your Own PR (£8.99)
___ Doing Business Abroad (£10.99)
___ Doing Business on the Internet (£12.99)
___ Doing Voluntary Work Abroad (£9.99)
___ Emigrate (£9.99)
___ Employ & Manage Staff (£8.99)
___ Find Temporary Work Abroad (£8.99)
___ Finding a Job in Canada (£9.99)
___ Finding a Job in Computers (£8.99)
___ Finding a Job in New Zealand (£9.99)
___ Finding a Job with a Future (£8.99)
___ Finding Work Overseas (£9.99)
___ Freelance DJ-ing (£8.99)
___ Freelance Teaching & Tutoring (£9.99)
___ Get a Job Abroad (£10.99)
___ Get a Job in Europe (£9.99)
___ Get a Job in France (£9.99)
___ Get a Job in Travel & Tourism (£8.99)
___ Get into Radio (£8.99)
___ Getting a Job in America (£10.99)
___ Getting a Job in Australia (£9.99)
___ Getting into Films & Television (£10.99)
___ Getting That Job (£8.99)
___ Getting your First Job (£8.99)
___ Going to University (£8.99)

___ Having a Baby (£8.99)
___ Helping your Child to Read (£8.99)
___ How to Study & Learn (£8.99)
___ Investing in People (£9.99)
___ Investing in Stocks & Shares (£9.99)
___ Keep Business Accounts (£7.99)
___ Know Your Rights at Work (£8.99)
___ Learning to Counsel (£9.99)
___ Live & Work in Australia (£12.99)
___ Live & Work in Germany (£9.99)
___ Live & Work in Greece (£9.99)
___ Live & Work in Italy (£8.99)
___ Live & Work in Portugal (£9.99)
___ Live & Work in the Gulf (£9.99)
___ Living & Working in America (£12.99)
___ Living & Working in Britain (£8.99)
___ Living & Working in China (£9.99)
___ Living & Working in Hong Kong (£10.99)
___ Living & Working in Israel (£10.99)
___ Living & Work in New Zealand (£9.99)
___ Living & Working in Saudi Arabia (£12.99)
___ Living & Working in the Netherlands (£9.99)
___ Living Away From Home (£8.99)
___ Making a Complaint (£8.99)
___ Making a Video (£9.99)
___ Making a Wedding Speech (£8.99)
___ Manage a Sales Team (£8.99)
___ Manage an Office (£8.99)
___ Manage Computers at Work (£8.99)
___ Manage People at Work (£8.99)
___ Manage Your Career (£8.99)
___ Managing Budgets & Cash Flows (£9.99)
___ Managing Credit (£8.99)
___ Managing Meetings (£8.99)
___ Managing Projects (£8.99)
___ Managing Your Personal Finances (£8.99)
___ Managing Yourself (£8.99)
___ Market Yourself (£8.99)
___ Mastering Book-Keeping (£8.99)
___ Mastering Business English (£8.99)
___ Master GCSE Accounts (£8.99)
___ Master Public Speaking (£8.99)
___ Migrating to Canada (£12.99)
___ Obtaining Visas & Work Permits (£9.99)
___ Organising Effective Training (£9.99)
___ Pass Exams Without Anxiety (£7.99)
___ Passing That Interview (£8.99)
___ Plan a Wedding (£8.99)
___ Planning Your Gap Year (£8.99)
___ Preparing a Business Plan (£8.99)
___ Publish a Book (£9.99)
___ Publish a Newsletter (£9.99)
___ Raise Funds & Sponsorship (£7.99)
___ Rent & Buy Property in France (£9.99)
___ Rent & Buy Property in Italy (£9.99)